ABOUT SICILY

Travellers in an Ancient Island

David D. Hume

J. N. TOWNSEND PUBLISHING
EXETER, NEW HAMPSHIRE
1999

Second Printing, 2007.
Printed in Canada.

Published by:
J. N. Townsend Publishing
PublishingWorks, Inc.
60 Winter Street
Exeter, NH 03833
603/778-9883

Sales:
Revolution Booksellers, LLC
60 Winter Street
Exeter, NH 03833
1-800-REV-6603
www.revolutionbooksellers.com

ISBN-13: 978-1-880158-24-1

Library of Congress Cataloging-in-Publication Data
Hume, David D., 1928-
About Sicily: travellers in an ancient island / David D. Hume.
p. cm.
1. Sicily (Italy)--Description and travel. 2. Hume, David D., 1928- I. Title.
DG864.3 H86 1999
914.5'804929--dc21   99-35603
                                                 CIP

ABOUT SICILY

*"...Sicily is an island lying outside time, where past events endure
in an eternal present, a beach on which the tides of successive civilizations
have heaped in disorder their assorted treasure."*
—*from* The Golden Honeycomb *by* Vincent Cronin

CONTENTS

AUTHOR'S NOTE

Our first adventures of Italian travel were in northern Italy. We visited the cities where the new learning and arts of the Renaissance flourished in the valleys of the Arno, the Po and the Adige. For some years we put off visiting the south, where we knew there was another rich and far older culture on the mystical, desperate, honey-colored island of Sicily. At first we were inhibited from going there in the face of the tales of lawlessness and organized crime. We got over our anxiety. It turned out that the three-cornered island is very kind to tourists and was quite protective of us. Armed with a slightly greater knowledge of Italian than we had on our earlier trips, we had the opportunity to meet people and even come to know some well enough to have maintained friendships over the years since. It became clear to us that with the use of a handful of phrases and a willing attitude, any American can get on happily in Sicily in economical lodgings or in high style. While visiting this island any traveler will experience an enormous repository of history, and encounter amazing works of medieval art, Baroque architecture, and the best monuments of the civilization of classical Greece to be found standing today. And the food is robust, delicious and inexpensive.

I am indebted to Sigmund Diamond for advice, encouragement and the use of his extensive library of the history and art of the Mediterranean. I have drawn on many books that concern the long and bloody struggle of the southernmost Italians to achieve their own destiny, from the wars of pre-Roman antiquity to the Sicilian Vespers and the Risorgimento.

My wife Cathy has contributed much to this book by keeping detailed journals wherever we have gone, as well as encouraging me to write this account of our circuit of the island. Together we hope that our enjoyment in experiencing this magical place in the southern sea will help convince others that it is a wonderful destination for tourists if they have the curiosity to sample its history and stand in awe before its ancient temples and pious mosaics, its sparkling harbors, sunny beaches and chilly mountaintops.

D.D.H.
Wilmington, North Carolina
Salem, Connecticut
1999

Mary enthroned with Archangels, Monreale. The angels' costumes are similar to the ceremonial robes of the Byzantine emperors.

I.

ROGER II

The Palatine Chapel exploded on our sight, a myriad of tiny golden lights, millions of mosaic bits of stone and glass forming patterns and pictures in brilliant colors against a gold and silver background. Above our heads, all images were dominated by a strong, sad face of Christ Pantocrator, the Lord and Maker of all, covering the full curve of the small apse, regarding us, mortal objects of his affection, with solemn concern. Above us protruded the gilded wooden stalactites of an African Islamic ceiling, surrounding a modest dome that presented another Christ staring directly down on us. And all around him circle eight archangels whose blue and white wings seem to float out from the background of the deep gold and silver stone tesserae.

The amazing little room is only half the size but more than half again as old as the Sistine Chapel in Rome. Far distant from that future masterwork of the Renaissance, this place speaks from the very heart of the medieval world. From nearly nine centuries ago these depicted faces of Christ do not seem to find fault with our moral stature. The forbidding upraised hand of Michelangelo's judge of the quick and the dead is absent here. This Christ may be saddened by human weakness or human cruelty, but he is not vindictive or threatening. Here Roger II, first king of Sicily, built his palace and a chapel where he could hear mass from a throne placed higher than any other place except the altar itself. Even the bishop's seat was a few inches less exalted than that of the newly minted monarch. He seems to have been devout in his belief, but not very devoted to the authority of the pope from whom he received his royal title.

The king may have repented of butchering the innocent in his war to complete the conquest of Sicily and hold his dominions on the Italian mainland, but if he prayed for forgiveness here it was from a position that held such firmness necessary to complete the Lord's work. In the nearby church of the Martorana he is depicted as inclining his body ever so slightly while Christ Himself lightly places the crown upon Roger's head.

The mosaics in the chapel were almost surely made by Greek craftsmen. The legends are in both Roman and Greek characters. The names of the artists who drew the enormous figures are unknown, but they seem to have been of the Orthodox communion, Christians excommunicated by Pope Leo IX in 1024, less than a hundred years before the mosaics were made. The merging of the doctrinal and artistic traditions of eastern and western Christianity gave Sicily a richer texture and a more lavish background for display of the majesty of her new sovereign. The Normans were Roman Catholics, but not so devotedly Roman that they would forgo imprisoning the Pope when there was an opportunity to exact ransom along the way. Roger I, who became known as "The Great Count" of Sicily, and his uncle Robert "The Guiscard" had set out for adventures in the south at the end of the eleventh century. They were descendants of Tancred de Hauteville of Normandy. This was about the same time as their countryman William, who conquered the English in 1066. They had taken Rome, captured the pope, let him go and moved on to the south. There the deHautevilles found an island controlled by a loosely federated nobility of Saracens from North Africa who had held it for almost three hundred years. Their conquest was not a particularly bloody one. It took place before the First Crusade of Pope Urban II who decreed it a virtue to slay the infidel.* When the island was secure, Robert went back across the narrow strait of Messina and made himself lord of Calabria. Count Roger stayed on in Sicily to its eventual benefit.

The brilliant room, his son Roger II's palace chapel, was decorated with these instructive mosaic images to teach scripture to the worshipers by presenting the complete story of

---

*This extraordinary idea was a great change in church doctrine, which for a millenium had condemned slaughter of heretics. Worse was to come in later centuries.

the creation of man and woman, of their disobedience, their loss of innocence and their eventual redemption. There are mosaic illustrations of almost all of the scenes of Genesis. At the corners below the central dome the Evangelists stand solemnly in little arches of brilliant color. Matthew, Mark, Luke and John are accompanied by their traditional symbols of the Ox, the Lion, the Eagle and the Angel. Surrounding their images are arched inscriptions of the first words of each gospel: Latin on the outside, Greek within. Lower down, in other parts of the chapel, are mosaic inscriptions in Arabic characters as well. This blazing array of stone pictures was intended to make the bible stories clear to a congregation of many peoples and many beliefs. Adamo and Eva shield their nakedness with small leaves while the serpent slithers through the grass at their feet. A youthful but severe God the Father holds out a hand to them while he explains their punishment. Saints and angels crowd the long-legged arches. Mary places a solemn-faced Christ child in an ornate manger while mounted kings approach from the left and simultaneously present their gifts from the right. Joseph sits to one side with a look of puzzlement on his handsome, white-bearded face. A serving maid pours bath water into a golden basin while another Mary tests the temperature with her hand while balancing her naked baby on her knee. The star of Bethlehem glows golden above the angels, and the spirit pours forth from the heavens like a narrow pale blue cascade onto the head of the baby. This nativity scene stands out against a green background. The floor below is dark red, white and green marble intarsia. Blended from the work of three cultures, the chapel is a wondrous mixture of devotion and opulence.

It should be. Its builder was the most powerful sovereign in Europe and his capital, Palermo, was the largest city in the West.

This extravagant fountain stands in the Piazza Praetoria, in front of police headquarters. Done by Francesco Camilliani in 1554 for a Florentine-Spanish high roller, it was eventually sold to the Council of Palermo for the staggering price of 30,000 golden scudi. The 644 pieces of stone were brought by sea and reassembled in the piazza, which was rearranged to accommodate the fountain. The locals dubbed it the "Fountain of Shame" largely, I think, because of the embarrassed gestures of the principal figures.

II.

PALERMO

The name suggests a place both strong and languid, a realm of beauty and brutality. It housed the courts of centuries-old Greek, Carthaginian and Arab refinement before the first rough Norman adventurers overran it in the eleventh century. They rebuilt the town with defenses styled after the hard stone castles and churches of their northern tradition. Palermo was an old city even then. The Sicels for whom the island is named built a seaside town long before the beginning of the first millennium. Phoenicians from the far eastern end of the Mediterranean had long ago established their city at the foot of Mount Pellegrino. Carthaginians had been there as early as the sixth century B.C. Greeks and Romans came to enjoy its climate and the fertile *Conca d'Oro,* the "Golden Shell" in which the city basked for many fruitful centuries before the Vandals and Goths took it over from a declining Rome. Byzantine Greeks succeeded the barbarians by the fifth century A.D. They made a capital in Palermo but surrendered it more easily to the invading Saracens in the seventh century A.D. than did their hapless relatives in Siracusa. Tax incentives for converts had encouraged much of the population to embrace Islam by the time the Normans "rechristianized" the island in the years after 1100.

Roger II de Hauteville, first to use the title King of Sicily, was an unusual man and an unusual Christian for his era. He acquired the title from Anacletus, a Pope of questionable legitimacy. As a result of a bargain with the pontiff, he also got the right to nominate bishops as the local apostolic legate. This was a great power in a time of slowly growing papal authority elsewhere. It gave Roger the means to govern without the more usual fragmentation of the feudal system. All land ownership was owed directly to the king's bounty. Although the Normans had been anarchic freebooters in recent generations before his time, he established a centralized and meticulously organized kingdom where he presided over the most civilized court in Europe. It became the site of an effective collaboration among soldiers, bureaucrats, clergy and scholars of Roman, Orthodox and Islamic belief or background. Some historians credit him with inventing the first modern European state, a unified country with a standing army, a secretariat and a bureaucracy, which brought all authority to his seat of government. The rest of Europe was fragmented in feudal organization (or lack of it) for another half millennium. Surely he was one of the most tolerant of monarchs, allowing all religions more or less free practice in his realm. Moslems and Jews wore a distinguishing badge but were otherwise allowed far greater freedom than in any other country of his century. Non-Christians were governed and judged by their own laws. As the slowly growing "reconquista" gathered force in Spain, more and more of the non-Christian scholars of Iberia emigrated to Sicily. Scholarship, science, the poetry of love songs, and art all flourished in Palermo in the time of Roger II, and continued throughout the reigns of the deHauteville dynasty and its successors, the Swabian house of Frederick II.

But along with Norman order and prosperity, much violent history also seems concentrated in Palermo, currently a city of three quarters of a million people surrounded by oranges, perfumed by flowers too rare for northern Europe, and decorated by extravagant Baroque churches and provocative sculptures celebrating life, love and desire. The greatest of Byzantine mosaics and the bold extravagance of Arab-Norman architecture decorate the city with an exuberant love of life and happy affirmation of human affinity. Love songs and mandolin tunes seem as natural to this city as the clash of arms or the more modern rattle of gunfire. Palermo in its time has heard much of all of these very human interactions.

With some sense that we were venturing into a dangerous territory, Cathy and I had reviewed our few phrases of Italian and boarded a plane from Rome. The flight was reassuringly civilized. A bit over an hour later we descended over the Tyrrhenian Sea through alternate bands of cloud and sun. We could see the *Porto* with its huge piers, protective seawalls and ferry docks whence boats for Africa and northern Italy put out. Always a sea town, Palermo saw the galleys of the

Punic Wars come from Rome more than 2,200 years ago, and also saw the ships of the Crusaders depart for the Levant more recently—only nine centuries before our own time. It also saw a few stragglers limp home in the ensuing centuries, when Islam reclaimed the Holy Land. Port towns are always melting pots and often places of social and religious toleration, where people of different cultures are happy to get along with each other while they engage in the prosperity of trade. It takes all sorts to make a harbor town, and Palermo has them all: pimps, poets, dramatists, criminals, saints, sculptors, honest cops, corrupt officials, the greatest cooks, crooks, carvers, and painters and the most intrepid sailors.

We entered the city itself from the airport at Punta Raisi by taking the bus for a fare of 5,000 lire, the equivalent of $3 for each of us. The obliging *autista* guiding the bus assured us he would tell us when we reached the Piazza Ruggero Settimo, before taking the remaining passengers farther on down the Via Maqueda to the railroad Termini. Halfway between these two bus stops, along the line of the Via Cavour, the city is divided between the old town of narrow and twisting streets and a newer area of broad avenues and fashionable shops. We were unencumbered by luggage since our bags had failed to make the transfer from the USAirways flight to Rome to the Alitalia plane for Sicily.* We strolled among carefully culti-

---

*This always seems to happen to us and we have ceased to worry about it. If you leave your bags unlocked the airline people will check them through customs for you and deliver them to your hotel the following day. We always carry a flight bag with a change of underwear and socks and our two toilet kits so we merely arrive in the new country less burdened than when we left home.

vated palm trees, stopped by the tourist bureau in the neighboring Piazza Castelnuovo, picked up an excellent map of the city, and went happily on across the broad sunny square towards the Politeama opera house. Mid-March weather in Sicily turned out to be just fine, sunny and cool. In our previous Italian travels we had never been able to find an opera company performing in any town while we were there. But here in Palermo were fresh new posters announcing Donizetti's *Daughter of the Regiment* for that very night. The box office was open and there were two seats in the geometrical center of the third balcony, seemingly waiting for us. 50,000 lira each for the tickets sounded like more than it really is in comparison with opera in the U.S.; $58 for two seats would never grant us admission to an opera in a major U.S. city. We pounced on them.

Even though most of the touristic sights are in the older quarter, we had decided to investigate the Hotel Petit or the Albergo Principe di Belmonte partly because of their modest prices for a double with a shower (65,000 lira, less than $40 at the time*) and partly becasue *The Lonely Planet Survival Guide: ITALY* said nice things about one of them and

---

*The lira hovered around 1,600 to the dollar during our first trip to Sicily. At this rate, 100,000 lire is worth slightly more than $62. Later voyages found the dollar worth as much as £1,750: around $57 to £100,000. We adopted the strategy of multiplying prices in lire by six, rounding out and inserting the decimal point wherever it made sense; thus a 6,000 lire *piatto* of spaghetti costs $3.75; a 25,000 lire silk scarf is only $15; a three-star hotel room at 175,000 lire comes to $105; and twenty million for a new Fiat is about $12,500. Assuming that you can do this sort of math in your head, I have quoted most prices in lire hereafter. Conversion to the Euro is simpler, about 1.10 to the dollar just now.

Let's Go Italy commented on the other, while mentioning that the neighborhood was both safe and "crowded with cafes." Since we had to select an address for the bags to catch up with us, we chose the latter hotel sight unseen. Both hotels are small and located near the diagonal corners of a little park down the slope from a pedestrian mall that has been created by prohibiting cars from three blocks of the Via Principe di Belmote. That sloping street has a number of pleasant bars of the Italian sort, providing everything from breakfast to afternoon tea, an aperitivo, or a late-night drink. The hotel was something of a surprise since it turned out to start on the fourth floor of a slightly dingy office building (*terzo piano*, or third storey, by the continental method of counting floors). Although it was shortly after seven in the morning and we had gotten precious little sleep on the plane overnight. We were just in time to indulge in that honorable Italian custom of a pleasant *pisolino* or nap after lunch.

Inexpensive hotels in Sicily require a certain attitude of combined delight and demand on the part of the customer. We have stayed at the Principe di Belmonte on two occasions. The first time all was in good order even though the tariff seemed very low. But on a later occasion at the same hotel we were given the last room available (we had arrived too early) and a few things had to be adjusted. The mattress was lumpy, the bedspring had a wild loose prong that came up through the bedclothes, the light on the nightstand was inoperable, the room was very cold, the water heater hanging in an upper corner over the bathroom sang like a teakettle five minutes out of every twenty, there was no teleremote for the TV set, the shower lacked a curtain, and I needed a second pillow for my stiff neck.

We brought these problems to the attention of Pietro, the *facchino*, or number one boy, before even troubling Rosario, the *proprietario*. The result was *stufa* (electric heater) for the chill, a new mattress, a different television set, bulbs for the lights, several extra pillows and the promise of a better room in another day. A shower curtain still with packing wrinkles was hung, and lots of towels provided. For the nonce we had to live with the noisy but effective water heater. Sicilians are the most obliging people in the world, but you do sometimes have to ask. Anyway, at less than $40 a night you have to make some compromises with what you might expect of a Hilton Hotel. For a bit more than twice the price of the Principe you could put up at the Albergo Mediterraneo in considerably greater style. As in all the Italy, three stars is up to anybody's reasonable standard, while a "two," although clean and safe, may require some sense of adventure.

Coming to Sicily for the first time was, of course, supposed to be an adventure for us. Every guidebook we looked at gave ominous advice about avoiding street crime, pickpockets and what Neapolitans call *scugnizzi*, child criminals of amazing skill and daring. Everyone will advise you not to let a preadolescent girl or boy stand next to you in a crowded location anywhere in the cities of southern Italy, especially on buses. But we discovered that with passports and wallets buttoned to the inside lining of our clothing in special interior pockets, we felt perfectly secure. Palermo, for instance, is certainly no more dangerous than New York or San Francisco if you follow a sensible regimen of not venturing into unlighted streets or waterfront saloons late at night. Sicily's reputation for being a dangerous place has never appeared remotely justified during our visits. Everyone we interacted with was helpful and kind to confused travellers, and on one occasion we were pursued into the street by a shop clerk to return to us an excessively large banknote that we had mistakenly left with our payment.

We did take the trouble to learn a bit more Italian before we went, especially a few resounding expressions of disapprobation or the desire to be left alone. "Vattene!" is the Italian equivalent of "Beat it" or "Buzz off!" and said to be effective for the young, although we never had to use such verbal armament. We also had been told that bad as the Mafia is, its members are generally protective of tourists in Sicily. They own, or "protect," enough of the facilities that tourists might frequent that it has been in the interest of the forces of *Cosa Nostra* to ensure our safety. But don't joke about the Mafia in Sicily; the restaurateur or hotelkeeper may well be paying a fee to the mob, and thus is in effect a member. We were not trading in narcotics and also had decided to stay out of the sailors' red-light district. We felt quite safe and had no trouble at all in Palermo or any other town in Sicily. Later, in Siracusa, we once took to hitchhiking across the city when stranded by tardy Sunday morning bus service, something I would not dare to do in a large American city. Sicilians were kind to us wherever we went.

First among the great sights of Palermo besides the Cappella Palatina is the Cathedral of the Abbey of Monreale, actually some ten kilometers out of the center of the city, standing on a hill overlooking the *Conca d'Oro*. The sloping plane of the "Golden Shell" was named for the orange and lemon trees that were brought from Africa by the Saracens. Today this marvelous orchard area is much overspread by the growth of the city, and Monreale is now really connected by suburbs to Palermo itself.

King Roger II established a hunting preserve at Monreale. His son William the Bad made it a favorite residence, and King Roger's grandson, William the Good, established the Abbey. When he did so he used the authority of being Apostolic Legate that his grandfather had secured from an earlier pope, and raised the abbot to the rank of a metropolitan archbishop. William began the cathedral in 1174 and, in an amazing burst of fiscal and architectural energy, poured so much of the money of his kingdom into the construction of the church that it was substantially completed in only ten years. It was an extraordinary feat, undertaken partly because it helped center the authority of the church in western Sicily where the king was present, rather than in Messina or Siracusa, where there were other bishops less firmly under his control. The disintegration of the Roman Empire had left local bishops as the principal civil authorities. Roger's new sort of state effectively reversed the trend in Sicily.

It was nearly midday when we arrived at Monreale and we fortified ourselves at a pizzeria amid a laughing crowd of schoolgirls: seventh-graders, judging from the lack of inhibition of their giggles. They were seeking similar nourishment. Almost all the great sights of Italy are busily frequented by the young and their teachers. There are so many works of art and ancient buildings in every Italian city that just getting a working knowledge of the mother country is a major part of the standard elementary and secondary school curriculum. As I recall, the pizza was unimpressive if cheap, perhaps a justified warning that grownups should eat in more pricey establishments than those frequented by kids on a field trip.

When we first entered the great nave we hardly gave a serious glance to the tall bronze doors of the abbey church. They are of such rugged simplicity of design that I thought they must be modern additions, but in checking with the *Blue Guide* (usually a good thing to do sooner or later) I learned that they were done in the twelfth century by artists from mainland Italy. Unusual for this period, the makers' names are known because they signed their work: the West Doors by Bonnano da Pisa, the North Doors by Barisano da Trani. Flanked by stone jambs decorated in patterns of leaves, chevrons and other abstract symbols, the doors are topped by arches carved in simple geometrical patterns in stone and mosaic. Both portals mix Islamic abstraction with the north European love of storytelling in relief. The figures of Old and New Testament stories are clearly delineated in over forty rectangular panels on the main west doors. Each scene has its caption in bold Roman capital letters in a mixture of medieval Latin and early vernacular Italian, clearly meant to be read by all who enter here. Literacy was not solely for clerics at the court of the deHauteville kings of Sicily.

Once inside, the size of the church is far more impressive than when judged by the rugged simplicity of the Norman exterior. The nave and apse are together almost 340 feet long. The main altar is dominated by a semicircular half dome that displays still another image of Christ the all-powerful Pantocrator. His immense, sorrowful face must measure a dozen feet from top to bottom. The walls glow with thousands of square feet of mosaic tiles in gold, silver and colored stone. It reminded us strongly of the Palatine Chapel, but everything here is on a far greater scale, three or four times larger than in Roger's earlier construction.

In a church as big and as old as Monreale it is inevitable that "improvements" have been made by other artists in the styles of other times. But here the upper courses of the mosaics, although repaired during several centuries, are mostly to be seen in their original conception by the unknown Greek artists who made them eight centuries ago. *Adamo* and *Eva* are here again, their well-muscled bodies giving witness perhaps as much to the innocence of the artist as to our first parents, for his work displays a lack of knowledge of youthful female anatomy that could only have come from an upbringing of visual chastity. Eva's breasts lack aureoles and their nipples seem to be hanging from the very bottom of her bosom. Her rectus abdominis muscles would do credit to a welterweight boxer.

The extent of the mosaics on walls and arches is breath-taking. The guidebook says that there are 35,000 square feet of mosaic here, putting this church in the same league as Hagia Sophia in Constantinople and quite a bit larger than any of the great mosaic churches of Ravenna in northern Italy. One difference from the earlier examples of making huge pictures from bits of broken stone is the great amount of writing in the mosaics of Monreale. Each scene has its brief explanatory text in bold Roman capital letters. The great figure of the Pantocrator holds a book in his left hand, turned towards us so that we may read the open pages proclaiming the text, "I AM THE LIGHT OF THE WORLD. FOLLOW ME..." with a few tildes and abbreviations in the Latin of the left-hand page. On the right page a text in Greek capitals appears, presumably giving that same instruction to the Orthodox members of the congregation.

There is a wealth of human detail in the mosaics. The friends of Lazarus who are in the act of removing the stone cover of his coffin hold their noses with their fingers or with a handkerchief to ward off the stink that his sisters have warned the Lord about. Peter in Gethsemane seems to be performing surgery on the ear of the High Priest's servant, as Judas kisses Jesus and the soldiers reach to lay hands upon him. Nicodemus prepares to use a large pair of bolt cutters to cut off the heads of the nails that fix Christ's feet to the cross.

William II is depicted in the mosaics of Monreale twice, wearing the same costume of richly brocaded blue and gold material, but in quite different postures. In one he is seen genuflecting before the Virgin Mary, holding the great church in his hands and presenting it to the Mother of God. In the more centrally located portrait he is standing erect beside an enthroned Christ, who is firmly settling a magnificent crown on the monarch's head.

The cloister of Monreale is a lush garden ringed with hundreds of mosaic-encrusted, carved, and intaglio columns. The legions of capitals are all different. They seem to have been carved by six or seven master sculptors who spent many years decorating the abbey. Their style is not related to that of the Greek mosaicists who decorated the church itself. These artists work in the tradition of Provençal Romanesque sculpture. William obviously followed the family tradition of eclecticism in art as well as religious toleration. The cloister garden with its exotic plantings, decorated stonework and a little fountain on a pedestal in one corner, gives a north African, Islamic or Spanish feeling to this place designed for monkish contemplation.

Back in the city we briefly visited the cathedral of Palermo itself but found it less exciting than Monreale, simply because so many of the "improvements" made by powerful and pious leaders, both temporal and spiritual, have almost completely obscured all signs of its original Norman design. We tarried briefly to pay our respects to the tombs of both Roger II and his remarkable grandson, Holy Roman Emperor Frederick II, whose impact on Sicily we were to witness many times during our visits.

The central crossroads of downtown Palermo is the

Quattro Canti, the four corners, where the Corso Vittorio Emanuele intersects the Via Maqueda. The Baroque facades of the buildings on the corners are elaborate pieces of exuberant sculpture but are, unfortunately, so blackened by modern automobile pollution that they are barely noticeable unless you pause with purpose to examine them. North of the four corners the Via Maqueda and the Via Roma are modern one way avenues lined with sophisticated stores.

After a brief glance at the famous self-conscious nudes around the somewhat abused "Fountain of Shame" across from Police Headquarters, we found the day too far spent for further visits to works of art or history but still much too early for the seven thirty or eight o'clock dinner hour of any proper Sicilian *ristorante.* We took a bus up Via Roma and set out to locate Roney, a fashionable tea room recommended by the *Lonely Planet* guidebook.

Walking on north past the Teatro Politeama we discovered that the posters in front of the opera house had changed: Handel's *Agrippina* was scheduled for our last night in Palermo. Feeling quite grand while contemplating it, we checked the box office and found that tickets were less expensive than for Donizetti and there were a few seats left in the upper circle. The cast included a famous soprano, and the production had been designed by Franco Zeffirelli. It took very little persuasion to convince us that we deserved to go to the 6:30 performance, our second opera in four days.

Roney turned out to be located on the Via della Libertà just to the north of the beginning of that elegant tree-divided boulevard. It is a stylish example of that very Italian institution, the *pasticceria*. Fashionably dressed Palermitani arrived for what looked to us to be a diet-shattering *dolce* of whipped cream and elaborately iced cakes and tarts shortly after five in the afternoon. Later we learned in conversation with a pair of well-dressed businesswomen (a "posturologist" and a teacher) that the five o'clock sugar fix is considered a finish to a midday main meal and that a simple supper will either be much later or perhaps omitted altogether. But the institutional *pasticceria* is also a cocktail lounge in Italy, and we were able to order a dietetic gin and tonic and watch the natives live it up on the whipped cream and *mascherponi*. With red plush cushions on bentwood chairs and with attentive waiters, Roney brings a touch of Paris or Vienna to this sophisticated southern city.

We were back at the Politeama on the following night among fur-coated and taxicab-delivered patrons of the arts. Baroque operas such as those Handel composed in the early eighteenth century are often thought to be a series of recitatives and arias pretty much unadorned by the passionate dialogue and action that we associate with Verdi and Puccini or even Wagner. But the Teatro Massimo company had used lavish and brilliant sets and a great deal of movement on stage to bring the older masterpieces to life in our time. What looked like a black marble floor reflected changing ranks of Roman columns, thrones and an elaborately draped Baroque gilded couch for the lovers' assignations.* The action was lively

---

*Subsequent to our visit, the huge Teatro Massimo opera house has reopened after many years of restoration. Opera will now be still more spectacular in Palermo.

enough to keep up with the elegant scenery and the music was heavenly. If the famous soprano seemed perhaps a touch beyond her finest years, the wonderful younger singers in the cast more than compensated. Opera is such a national indoor sport for all in Italy that it is unlikely that you will have anything but a superb night at the theater if you are fortunate enough to find it presented in any city you are visiting.

Late in the evening (for Handel's idea of a proper opera takes close to five hours) we found our way to a pleasant little restaurant near the Politeama opera house, *Il Cancelletto Verdi,* where a post-theater dinner at 11 pm seemed quite the usual order of the day or night.

Palermo is a very civilized city today but it is, most of all, the location of the best and most extensive buildings of the wonderful if brief flowering of the Norman monarchy of Sicily. In the eleventh and twelfth centuries it was the premier capital of all western Europe and a political rival of Constantinople itself. As a matter of fact, Byzantium was captured for the first time and largely sacked not by Moslem Turks, but by marauding Norman crusaders of northern Europe in almost the same decade when William II was building the great abbey at Monreale. It is still a city full of great sights and pleasant adventures. Palermo's best times were surely under the rule of the deHauteville kings. Their eventual successor, Frederick II Hohenstaufen, the "Child of Apulia" who became Holy Roman Emperor, was known as *Stupor Mundi,* the "Wonder of the World." He became King of Jerusalem as well as King of Sicily and Holy Roman Emperor and reigned for close to fifty years, until 1250. His architecture was, however, mostly focussed on the needs of military organization. His octagonal towers still stand in Calabria and Puglia as well as parts of Sicily, removed from the residences of a nobility their presence was intended to dominate. The Swabian emperor may have exercised power from Sicily, but his was the final playing out of that dominion. In all, the Normans ruled Palermo for seven or eight generations. They are a formative influence there still.

Centuries later, while the Spanish Bourbons and the Austrians had their turns at dominating the triangular island, the wildest flowering of Baroque architecture and decoration took place in the interiors of churches and chapels in Palermo, especially in the startling stucco work of Giacomo Serpotta.

After the brilliantly displayed figures of Michelangelo and Bernini showed the way in the early sixteenth century, I thought that there was little novelty left to be revealed in three-dimensional studies of the nude or partially draped human body. But Serpotta was both an innovator and a master. He worked more rapidly than either of the two earlier masters of three-dimensional form. His figures were modeled in waterproof stucco with a sureness of design and cleanness of line that makes them look like chiseled marble with a softly finished surface. Stucco work of this remarkable artist dates from the last quarter of the seventeenth century to the earliest decades of the eighteenth. His facile modeling of the human figure shows up in many of the Baroque churches of

Palermo, perhaps most famously in the gracefully grisly stretching of St. Lawrence on the gridiron in the Oratorio di San Lorenzo. In pursuit of more examples of Baroque sculpture we entered the amazingly decorated church of San Ignazio di Olivella, where we found larger-than-life-sized apostles on each side of the sanctuary. Each figure is unique, bold and human, reminiscent of no other statue that we had ever seen. Each one is a masterpiece.

San Ignazio's church was also graced with the presence of a couple of charming young art historians or conservationists, who were measuring distances inside the church with great precision and recording their findings for future comparison with the possible alterations caused by earthquakes or the settling of the foundation. Their complimentary references to each other's specialties as well as many shared smiles gave us the impression that they were romantically as well as professionally linked. We later reflected that being young, in love, just on the threshold of a scholarly career in the study of such ancient beauty, and living in Sicily, must be like walking the very turf of Eden.

Archeology is so much around you in Palermo that it at first seemed almost superfluous to find a museum of prehistory in this city. We finally found it to our great advantage on our second visit. The Museo Archeologico Regionale is adjacent to San Ignazio and required a half day of rapid observation to give it scant justice. The surprising presence of Etruscan civilization (or trade with it) is much in evidence here. But the Greek ornamentation of the temples of Selinunte, both in tufa and in terra cotta, is the most impressive evidence of the pre-Christian era of Sicilian history. The metopes of a Greek temple are the panels between the three-ridged triglyphs in the architrave that rests on top of the capitals of the columns. In some early temples these metopes are plain, but in the most elaborately finished temples they are marvelous pieces of low-relief sculpture illustrating gods and heroes in the acts of their legends. The great temples of Selinunte have given up their best work of this sort to this museum in Palermo. The furious hounds of guilt attack Orestes here as they have for thousands of years. An embarrassed Odysseus beseeches a shy Nausicäa. Worn and fragmented though much of it is, it is worth the visit to give dimension to what you will see later at the site of the ruined temples themselves.

After this particular day of sightseeing among the works of the ancient Greeks, we worked our way back to Via Principe di Belmonte and discovered the Caffè Antiqua, a rather formally paneled *pasticceria* that looked a bit like a proper English ladies' club. The patrons were well if not opulently dressed, and a capable pianist provided a harmonious background. But a distinctly Italian note was struck by the presence of children, two girls aged about six and four, who rose from the table where their mothers were having tea and danced in graceful circles among the other guests to everyone's smiling approbation. We told the proprietor that we rated his establishment tops among the watering holes of Palermo, and he responded by giving us a handful of color photo postcards which showed the tearoom populated by a half dozen long-legged beauties, perched on the banquettes, displaying the top of the line of Milanese fashion, brief skirts and long legs. In his almost mystical analysis of Sicily in *The Golden Honeycomb*, Vincent Cronin points out that any art form that was imported to Sicily by its many foreign masters has inevitably been carried to a more extreme development here than in the country of its origin. The Greek temples are larger and grander than in Athens; the classical theaters are greater than those of the Greek mainland; the Norman churches outdo those of Normandy; the Spanish Baroque interiors go far beyond anything in Spain or northern Europe; the opera houses are gigantic. The same can be said of some of the examples of art deco design that have survived from the fascist era and escaped the bombings of World War II. Among these is the main post office and telecom building, which makes a clear and powerful statement about the authority of the state. At the head of the broad platform of steps facing the Via Roma, the facade of huge columns is a rank of smooth cylinders of poured concrete. The building looks a bit like Mussolini.

Palermo exhibits a great accretion of architectural styles—political, religious and utilitarian—somehow without losing the charm of its ancient streets, ubiquitous churches, statue-studded piazzas, patches of park and comfortable neighborhood bars and *pasticcerias*. It is, after all, the favorite city of the seafaring rat that tempted the countrified Ratty of *The Wind in the Willows* to come away with him to the south, beyond the green and leaping seas of the northern oceans and the

Channel to experience the very essence of the good life at the warm glowing jewel of the southern sea, the Kingdom of Sicily. The seafarer was a Norway Rat, surely related to the rats the Normans shipped with when the Guiscard and the other sons of Tancred de Hauteville came to the Mediterranean in the eleventh century.

Why has it taken so long for most of us to take up that beguiling invitation? What were we afraid of? There are many myths alive and palpable in Sicily, but the idea that it is unavoidably bristling with criminals is not true. We found more to believe in legends of nymphs and hamadryads dodging about her woodlands, or sirens tempting sailors to wreck themselves on her seductive shoreline.

Madonna and Bambino from the Palazzo Bellomo Museum, Sirracusa. Of the Gagini school, it is typical of the many Gagini sculptures in Sicilian churches.

III.

TO SEGESTA

Leaving Palermo to explore western Sicily means leaving the Middle Ages and entering a period either earlier or later than the Norman era of history and art. Far earlier invaders of Sicily came to the island almost two thousand years before the descendants of the Vikings came from northern Europe. The Phoenicians sailed from the eastern Mediterranean to establish colonies on the fabled triangular island. Later, other Punic descendants came from their greatest African colony, Carthage, less than a hundred miles from the western tip of the island. The connection with North Africa has been pretty much continuous ever since. In the later Middle Ages, Arabs ruled the whole of Sicily for 250 years before the Normans got there.

But by far the greatest colonizers of Sicily were the Greeks. No one is quite sure exactly when it started, but Corinth had made sizeable settlements in southeastern Sicily by the early eighth century B.C. The graceful ruins of their cities are everywhere on the southern side of the island, sometimes embedded in modern towns, sometimes in lonely places where only an occasional peasant passes the evidence of a vanished theater, market square or temple. Characteristically for the Greeks, the evidence of their domain and their passing is not in the ruin of palaces as it is in Myceneae or Crete. The Greeks, while not always democratic, were seldom monarchic and even their "tyrants," chosen as absolute rulers, sometimes for life, built few monuments to their own self-glorification or for luxurious living in the manner of the Persians or the Romans. Temples and theaters, gathering places for all the people, are the almost inevitable remains of a Greek colony. The Agoras of business or markets have left traces in some collections of ruins, but the columns of Doric-style temples are the most common signs of Greek occupation, and the semicircular rows of theater seats are the most durable.

To explore western and southern Sicily you don't absolutely have to have a car. Railroad and bus lines can bring young backpackers to even the smaller cities and almost all the great archeological sites. But being the age of having the leisure to visit the country as grownups made us decide that being masters of our own transportation is better and a lot easier than dragging our luggage on and off several trains a day and finding a place to check it at a rural railroad station. Even if having the car caused a slight upscaling of the economic pattern of previous trips, we decided we had earned it by the use of the low-cost hotel in Palermo. We arranged to rent an unknown vehicle from an unknown supplier by going through our U.S. travel agent to AutoEurope, the consolidator that had produced our bargain-priced tickets to Italy. We had received a voucher that covered the rental for unlimited miles and included all taxes including the VAT (which can run to as much as 18 or 20 percent in most European countries) and all necessary insurance. The voucher gave us an address in Palermo that was only three blocks from our hotel. It turned out to be the Avis agency. At $350 for ten days from a name-brand auto renter, it seemed to us to be a very good bargain.

The car was squeaky-clean, a new Fiat Punto with four doors, reasonable size and a tightly lockable trunk. We set forth up the Via Roma seeking a major cross street that would take us to the expressway to the west. Here we discovered that Palermitan drivers are among the most polite that we had ever encountered. There is a *semaforo* (traffic light) at fewer than a third of the street intersections; where the lights are lacking, all drivers slow to a halt or nearly so at each corner and look both ways before pressing on. This courtly tradition is amplified by the zebra-striped crossings where pedestrians have the right of way and you *must* stop if anyone on foot challenges you. Our progress was dignified if a bit slow. There is much nodding and smiling and waving of others through. It seemed a very agreeable change from Rome or even most mid-sized cities in the U.S. Our experience on our first day of driving in Sicily was borne out all over the island. With the dramatic exception of the city of Catania, Sicily is an agreeable and safe place to drive.

The A-29 runs north from Palermo past Monte
Pellegrino and turns west inside of the coastal promontory
of Monte Gallo. We passed our arrival point at the airport of
Punta Raisi and thence drove on parallel to the coast and a
series of small beach towns facing the deep blue of the Gulf
of Castellammare and the Tyrrhenian Sea. Out there, to our
right, lay the picture book island of Ustica. On our left was a
series of fantastic cliffs and rock formations five and six hundred feet high, saw-toothed ridges of grey stone that rose
from brilliant green foundations and faded into mistier colors of blue and purple toward their summits. The jagged and
uneroded crests give witness to the seismic activity of Sicily.
These hills are still young on a geologic time scale, just as the
traces of their inhabitants are very old by human measure.
The western hill country's first recorded people were the
Sicani; the earliest known eastern people were the *Siculi*. Both
groups were well established in Sicily between the fifteenth
and tenth centuries B.C., perhaps earlier. I wondered what
sort of crops they farmed in a country which must have been
largely wooded in that time. Today there are brilliant yellow
fields of the oilseed rape in the spring, as well as orange and
lemon orchards. In the age of the Roman empire the island
produced an enormous amount of wheat.

We were on our way to a famous site of religious devotion and commercial competition, which was built far earlier
than those of the Norman warrior kings we had visited in
Palermo. Sixty kilometers west of that city the road turned
inland and climbed between small mountains towards the

interior of the island. Our way on the excellent modern highway forked to the south and then took us through a tunnel onto an upland plateau, where we found modest signs pointing us to Segesta. We wound around a hill, down into a valley and up again, and suddenly saw for an instant the orange and brown silhouette of a classical temple pediment. Our ideas of Greek architecture had been so conditioned by the reproductions of Washington, D.C., and the color photographs of the Pentellic marble of Athens that we were surprised by the tawnier colors of the Sicilian temples. Originally pale cream in color, the volcanic tufa which was used for many of them has turned golden or tan with the years. This stone is softer than marble, but even so, it has withstood 2,500 years of wind and rain erosion here.

The approach to the Segesta temple is quite perfect and very dramatic. From a nearly empty *parcheggio* we walked up a diagonal path toward the lofty facade, passing between shoulder-high bushes of yellow and green wild *finocchio* (Florence fennel), the tops of the bushes looking like overgrown broccoli. On the slope there were little orange calendula blossoms and small violet flowers we later learned were called fabiana.

At the level summit of the hill we found ourselves still looking up a slight rise toward the solemn shell of the temple. There are six Doric columns across the front, thirty-six in the total perimeter, all still standing. The entablature and pediments are still in place, but inside it is empty and roofless. The great silence of the place was punctuated by the cries of hundreds of birds that roost on the capitals. For a time, while we walked silently among the columns, we were the only people there.

There are many ancient sites in Sicily that have been inhabited by succeeding peoples for many centuries, but the truly amazing ones seem to me to be those that have never been rebuilt and remain today standing in the wilderness. I am told that Morgantina is like this, but we have not yet visited it. Here at Segesta there remain the ruins of a theater and this one temple, magnificent in their isolation, bare relics of ruinous wars fought for settlement of long-forgotten quarrels twenty or more centuries ago. The temple is 180 feet long, and the 30-foot columns are more than 6 feet in diameter at their bases. Its elegance and size demonstrate a great sense of pride and purpose in a people whose other works have totally vanished. We don't know the names of anyone who lived here when the city flourished, or who worshipped in this splendid building. We aren't even sure of the name of the god or goddess in whose honor it was raised.

Because the fitting of the sections of the large columns of Doric temples required rotating the drums in place to grind them to a perfect fit, they could not be fluted before they were erected. The columns of the Segesta temple are still smooth, ungrooved, giving evidence that although the full circuit of columns is here, the temple was never quite completed. The absence of an inner temple chamber, the *cella,* would seem to bear this out. The city's growth and life ended at this climax of her flowering. The only sign of any other part of the city showing above ground now at Segesta is its theater, a well-preserved semicircle of the lower courses of stone seats where at one time more than 3,500 people could have formed the outdoor audience of the quasi-religious spectacle of the Greek tragedies. We have no record of the performances but it is likely that Sophocles, Euripides and the later Roman comedies of Plautus and Terence were acted here. The city was prosperous and allied itself with Carthage while making war on Selinunte, its rival on the south coast. But the Segestans did not remain loyal to their African allies. In the first Punic War, around 260 B.C., they slaughtered the Carthaginian garrison and joined the Roman cause. Segesta declined slowly during the Roman period, possibly for lack of access to the sea, for the Romans had learned to be sailors while contesting with Carthage. The site was abandoned in the early Christian era, and what was left did not survive the brief conquest of the Vandals in the declining years of Roman power in the unknown, dark-age era of the fifth and sixth centuries. Today it is an isolated, romantic reminder of the inevitable, eventual passing away of all sovereignty and the impermanence of the accomplishments of any civilization. I wonder what my New England village will look like in another couple of thousand years? Indianapolis? Mexico City? Bir-el-asli?

We had a pleasant lunch in the cafeteria and souvenir shop at the foot of the hill. The helpful concessionaire taught us the Linnean Latin names of some of the wildflowers that decorated the early spring of these upland hills. In all we didn't tarry more than two and a half hours in Segesta. But the sight of that lonely classical temple-front at the crest of the green hill, and the cries of the birds within, come back to me whenever I look at a monumental civic center at home, in Europe, or in Asia. Wise old Mr. Badger in *The Wind in the Willows* comments on the permanence of the animal communities that far outlast the cities of men and women: "You know how they are," he says to the Mole. "They come for a while and then they go away."

Gathering advice about entering Marsala against the grain of a one-way street.

IV.

MARSALA & ERICE

We turned off the A29 to the south before the road would lead us on to Trapani at the far west end of the island. The distance between the interior and the coasts of Sicily has always been disproportionately great for so small an island, but never greater than it became in the seventeenth and eighteenth centuries. The boundaries of the old Norman fiefs had by that time become areas of cloudy lineage owned by a mixed set of barons who owed a feudal allegiance to the King of the Two Sicilies, who was a Spanish Bourbon. He lived in Naples and never visited the island. His representative in governing the aristocracy was a viceroy who had little control over it. The method of selling Sicilian wheat through brokers operating under royal license enriched the brokers, helped the careless aristocracy slide into debt, and impoverished the peasants who grew the wheat. Taxes which made the poor pay as much per head as the rich were levied on foodstuffs. The city of Palermo, the clergy, and a few other interest groups were exempt from all taxes. The situation became a real motivation for a savage, French-style revolution in the years after 1789. The Queen even matched that chapter of history; she was Maria Carolina of Austria, the sister of Marie Antoinette of France, the queen who died under the guillotine.

But things didn't work out as savagely in Sicily as they did in France. As in many early revolutionary situations, an intellectual and liberal group of aristocrats tried to change things for the better but met with limited success. Among these high-minded but often ineffective leaders were the Principe di Belmonte and his uncle, Principe di Castelnuova, who had actually lived for a time outside of Sicily and seen the current cohesive and relatively efficient economy of England. An ineffectual constitution was enacted in 1812 with some British protective muscle behind it. It granted some rights of self-government but mostly to the nobles, and did about as much good for the peasants as Magna Carta did in England 600 years earlier. It did away with the forms of feudalism, the use of torture, and the inquisition, but had only limited economic impact on the poverty of the interior, where the greatest needs were land tenure for the actual farmers and roads to bring their produce to open markets. The great agricultural holdings of the barons, the *latifondi*, continued to be worked by a peasantry in virtual serfdom. Even the streams and rivers were owned by absentee lords whose greatest interest was in how grand their carriages and how magnificent their palazzi were in Palermo or its near suburbs, both of them tax-free zones for centuries.

The backwardness of the Sicilian economy in the eighteenth and nineteenth centuries is amazing. Sitting in the middle of the sea, they imported most of the fish they ate. They imported basic textiles made of Sicilian-grown fiber, and soap made elsewhere from their own fats and olive oil. The only explanation seems to be the combination of a regressive tax system, an almost total absence of an entrepreneurial class and easy bribery of customs officials. The island was sharply divided between a rich and feckless nobility, who spent everything they could grasp on elegance and show, and a desperately poor peasantry. Both had been taught to trust no one outside of the family and to hide any loose change under the mattress. The only loyalty was to the family. There was no investment, no insurance, no partnership and no venture capital. The guilds discouraged the development of skilled labor, and the nobility paid for the importation of nothing but luxury items, tobacco, coffee and perfume in preference to industrial money-making equipment. The aristocracy simply felt that business or industry were beneath them, as was the repayment of debt or taxes.

The country was not so much misgoverned by the Bourbon monarchy in Naples as it was ungoverned and left in the hands of private criminals and law evaders of all classes. Long before the Mafia, bribery and protection payments were necessary for anyone doing business.

Happily traversing the western quarter of Sicily in the spunky little car on a modern highway, we turned south again short of Trapani and drove through a flat coastal country where there are age-old lagoons for the evaporation of seawater for the manufacture of salt in the almost desert-dry air of the southern Mediterranean. The area seems neither particularly prosperous nor poor, but relatively unchanged and unchangeable in spite of the contesting armies that have swept through at frequent if irregular intervals throughout the millennia. We found our way into the old western town of Marsala by following our noses and the angle of the sun. There were not enough roads to choose from to present much confusion, and all the highways of Sicily are well posted with legible signs.

Marsala was battered by Allied bombing before the invasion of 1943. Acres of the old city were destroyed, and a fair amount of the area has never been rebuilt. Some neighborhoods and the entire western promontory of the city have been left deserted as a series of large archeological parks. Most of the architecture still extant above ground level is, with a few exceptions, undistinguished at best. The western tip of the city today is a series of green, rubble-strewn fields, occupied by a small Baroque chapel, a low-profile museum and a massive concrete cinema styled in the heavy fascist-era architectural idiom of the 1930s. The theater looks disused, and the grand sidewalks that lead to it are weedy and seem unfrequented. There is a handsome gateway alongside a tented restaurant and pizzeria that connects this rather vacant area with the crowded and narrow streets of the old town inside.

But the little museum on the oceanside is a fascinating place. Within the past twenty years underwater archeology has come into its own in the Mediterranean, and one of the oldest wooden artifacts recovered anywhere is a large chunk of a Carthaginian ship, almost precisely datable as having been built around 230 B.C. This was the time of the Second Punic War, just before the end of the third century B.C. when Rome fought with its Carthaginian rivals. This was the fateful conflict that featured Hannibal's elephants crossing the Alps and marked the beginning of Rome as a sea power, something Carthage had already been for centuries. Hundreds of ships were built by both sides during seventeen years of continuous war. The example found at Marsala is probably typical of most of them, although it is hard to tell from the remains whether it was a cargo carrier or strictly a warship. There was probably only a little difference between the types at the time.

About one-third of the length of one side of the vessel is preserved inside a humidity-controlled tent with large plastic windows. The ship timbers are shaped in a manner much like the method of construction the Scandinavians followed 1,200 years later: the vessel was planked from keel to gunwales first and the ribs inserted later, quite the opposite of wooden boatbuilding of the medieval European and more recent times. Wrought copper nails as well as amazingly unrusted iron fastenings, anchors, amphorae for carrying supplies, and all sorts of first-millennium nautical gear are on exhibition. Besides being artifacts of that historically crucial conflict, the museum exhibits show the extent to which the Mediterranean was a highway of commerce, most briskly frequented for the thousand years before the heyday of the Roman Empire. Although the hull is more recent than the ships of Odysseus and the Argives that found their way through these seas, scattered on their trip home from the war with Troy, its form and obviously traditional technology are evidence of this blue sea being studded with sails, a huge avenue of great commerce as long ago as the early kings of Knossos on Crete and the Pharaohs of the Middle Kingdom dynasties of Egypt. The Egyptians were never the navigators that the Phoenicians were or that the later Romans became, but from ancient times there were plenty of ships on this sea. Looking slightly south of west from this strand of Marsala, I could imagine the sight of the great single square sails and flashing oars of the war galleys and merchantmen crossing between Sicily and the promontory of Cap Bon in Tunisia, only ninety miles away. This ocean connects more than divides Sicily and Africa.*

Anywhere you stick a spade in the earth or drag a rake through the sea bottom in or near Sicily, you are likely to come up with the spoor of more than one civilization. We spent our second day on the west coast driving back north to Erice, near the more modern city of Trapani.†Going back north along the SS-115 (a good secondary road which skirts

---

*The name of the town (which the Greeks and Romans called Lilybaeum) comes from *Marsa-Allah*, "The Harbor of God," a title given by the Islamic conquerors who came to take it in the final declining years of the Romans, after the Vandals and the Byzantine Greeks had their way with it.

†Trapani is another of those exceptions to the usual pattern of penultimately accented place names. Hit the first *a*.

the entire south coast of Sicily) we passed the salt-producing flats again and regretted that we would not that day be able to take the turnoff to the lagoon on the west where the archaeologically active islet of Motya can be visited by a short ferry crossing. Continuing excavation here has brought up sculpture and ceramics from Phoenicia, Corinth, and perhaps even Mycenae. The island is owned by the legatees of an English winemaking family, the Joseph Whitaker Foundation, which encourages the research.

As we reached the southern fringe of Trapani the hazy sunshine began to clear and we suddenly saw a huge looming shape on the horizon far ahead. Along this flat coastline the appearance of a 2,400-foot mountain right on the sea is startling. On the top of this one was our goal, the medieval village of Erice. As we wound our way up a serpentine modern road toward the summit I wondered what economic production could have supported even a small village in such a location. The answer turned out to be the protection that the mountain afforded against attack by sea raiders. Today the presence of tourists and a few other visitors seem the only industry here. The town is old and once had a famous temple to the goddess of fertility, Venus Erycina, surely another good reason for a flourishing tourist trade. Having been captured more than once in the era of the Punic Wars, Erice prospered as the site of the Venus cult into the days of the early Roman emperors Tiberius and Claudius. After the Saracen period, Count Roger I renamed it Mount San Giuliano because he dreamt of Julian while besieging the hill. In a brief fit of classicism the *fascisti* put the old name back on the place in the 1930s.

It is said that Tunisia is visible on a clear day from the summit of Erice. The presence of the mountain itself was surely a good landmark for sailors crossing from Africa in the years before the lodestone compass, never mind Loran and SatNav. Today it is swept and garnished for the daily arrival of visitors and has plenty of little tea shops and small *ristorante*. This is the town where the famous Maria of *Bitter Almonds* plied her trade, and half the eating places in town use her name and sell the book as well as the confections it describes. We were assured that our luncheon spot was the locale of the real Maria's oven. Not ready to quibble about authenticity, we enjoyed the lunch.

Older books comment on the amount of red-to-blond hair in Erice's population of less than a thousand. We did not notice particular examples of this beguiling complexion, but I am willing to believe that there is shallow pool of Norman genes in this isolated town. People here are said to claim such ancestry with pride. Erice may have only 800 inhabitants, but like almost every Italian town, it has its own museum, the Biblioteca e Museo Comunale Cordici. Here, besides a small public library whose stacks we were allowed to browse without hindrance from the agreeable librarian, there are a number of local archeological finds, most notably a stunning Greek head of Aphrodite of the fifth century B.C. Here we also became aware for the first time of the work of Antonello Gagini, the founder of a dynasty of great Sicilian sculptors beginning in the *Quattrocento* and continuing into the early seventeenth century. Gian Domenico Gagini provided the most notable sculptures in Sicily in the sixteenth century. The early Gaginis were masters at creating delicately featured, almost adolescent Madonnas that grace churches in towns all over the island. Wonderful as their sculpture is, it seems somehow to have escaped the notice (or at least much of the commentary) of most of the describers of Italian works of art. Look for Gaginis wherever you go in Sicily, especially in the cathedral of Siracusa.*

Poking into the rear porch of what I took to be a church, we discovered ourselves in an almost modern remodeled lecture hall full of serious-looking people, most of them seemingly too old to be university students. I paused and listened to a few familiar sounds and discovered that the lecturer was speaking a language I could more or less understand.

"Between the spiral arms," he said with a thick Slavic accent, "there are still large amounts of unorganized dust and gas...."

We had climbed this mountain towards the sky and unwittingly joined the students of the heavens, an international seminar of astrophysicists. Although a number of the participants wore name tags that said they came from Russia, Hungary and Ukraine, they all seemed to share broken English as

---

*I eventually discovered reference to at least eleven Gaginis (without worrying about mere followers). I have generally made no serious attempt at differentiating them, since the style is remarkably coherent, even if at its best among the earlier members of the family.

the common tongue of science. It turns out that there have been regular conferences of physicists and their ilk here for many years. The street pavements of Erice seem unique to this triangular town. The stones are laid in a sort of "Fontainbleau Parquet" style, regular and of uniform size, but roughly shaped and obviously laid long ago by artisans following a traditional pattern. With its wonderful almond pastries, the medieval architecture, the sidewalks and the discourse of contemporary scientists, Erice is a small-scale stop of top quality. Even the food in the little touristic restaurants is quite good, although the taped music is a bit corny, consisting of current crooners doing the likes of *O Sole Mio* and *Funiculi-Funicula* with computer-tempo accompaniment. Oh well, all Italian tenors are fun to listen to, even the pop performers. The little mountaintop village with the long history is, after all, supported by the tourist trade today. It accommodates this well and with a style of its own.

Our return to Marsala gave us a feeling of coming home even though we had only arrived there the day before. We had found an exceedingly comfortable hotel rather by accident while asking directions as we passed around—and almost encircled—the old portion of the town. We looked for something designated as *tre stelle* (three stars), in order not to push the luck we had with the economical and pleasant two-star Principe di Belmonte in Palermo. We arrived at the Hotel President and found it to be a very modern building that had just opened a large four-story wing and added a newly tarmacked parking lot, which was occupied by less than a half dozen cars. The place reeked of luxury and looked as though it might claim a rating of at least four stars. We were wafted through a stately lobby and up to the largest hotel room we had ever hired in Italy. The tariff turned out to be a more or less affordable 140,000 lire, around $80 a night, bearable if we didn't stay too long. I was comforted to remember paying as much at a Holiday Inn "Express" in northern Florida.

Travel always convinces me that there are only 139 people in the world and they all know or are at least distantly related to each other. A tour bus arrived as we descended to seek our *aperitivo* and disgorged, among others, a couple whose sons I had the pleasure to have in school in prior years in New York. They were on a trip with the American Archeological Society (he as their volunteer legal counsel) and had just come from the south side of Sicily, where they had visited the full set of the great Greek sites we intended for the next week. There was something about sharing dinner with old friends met quite by chance in Marsala at the extremity of this ancient island that made me wonder which other of our friends or distant relatives might be lurking around the end of the next temple or castle, those we would *not* encounter because we turned in the other direction or decided to have lunch before rather than after touring the site.

Marsala's cathedral presents one of those surprising connections between different nations that show how Christendom was a seamless garment in the Middle Ages. Since the late twelfth century a series of churches have been built on this site and have come down in war and earthquake. All of them have been named San Tommaso di Canterbury, dedicated to the tough-minded, Italian-educated* Frenchman and friend of Henry II of England, who was murdered by the king's men in the belief that their sovereign wanted the bishop out of the way to settle the matter of the authority to invest bishops in England. They might have been right in their surmise, but Henry made a great demonstration of penitence that his hasty complaints had led to the martyrdom. Canterbury became one of the three greatest pilgrimage sites of the Middle Ages and the name of Saint Thomas à Becket graced churches all over Europe.

Sicily and England had a great affinity in the twelfth and thirteenth centuries and again in the eighteenth and nineteenth; perhaps it had something to do with the Norman and later Angevin dynasties at first. Later it centered around control of the Mediterranean, and the English taste for the fine wines of Marsala. The son of Henry II was Richard I, who was known as Cœur de Leon because, like most English Normans, the Lion Heart spoke more French than English. Somehow the English royals never got the hang of learning the languages of the countries they conquered the way their Sicilian fellow travellers did. Richard's younger sister was married to the young prince who became William II, known as The Good, but she died young

---

*Like so many lawyers of the Middle Ages, Thomas à Becket took his LL.B from the University of Bologna

and childless, as did her handsome husband. Richard stopped by Messina on his way to his courtly if less than successful crusade against Saladin in the east. He caused all sorts of mischief in Sicily while trying to get a refund of his deceased sister's dowry. On his way back home from Palestine, he was captured while traveling down the Rhine by a vassal of the Hohenstaufen emperor and held for ransom; thence Robin Hood, the Sheriff of Nottingham and all that trouble with bad King John. It seems ironic that the one collecting the ransom was the father of Frederick, who through his mother was born King of Sicily because his cousin William (The Good) had been unsuccessful in getting his English queen (sister of the captive) with child. Oh well, it's all in the family.

The mother church of Marsala thus has a long history, but unfortunately little architectural splendor to show for it. It has a nice Baroque facade that originated in the seventeenth century, but much of the church collapsed in 1893 for reasons I have been unable to determine. It was rebuilt in recent memory. There is a nice little piazza in front where the young and old of the city gather during the late afternoon *passeggiata,* or walkabout, when cars are excluded from the center of town. This agreeable event happened to coincide with our first attempt to enter the town by car.

But while a little disappointed by the period of the church and the roundabout route we had to take to get to it, we were rewarded by exploring behind it on the Via Garraffa and finding the small Museo degli Arazzi, the museum of the tapestries. It contains just eight wall hangings. These were given to the cathedral in 1589 by Antonio Lombardo, Archbishop of Messina, who showered his largesse on his hometown by providing this set of remarkable works of art, which he somehow picked up while he was ambassador to Spain in the late sixteenth century. They were woven in Brussels and are masterworks of the weaver's art, depicting a set of scenes purporting to show the conquest of Jerusalem by the Roman emperor Titus. The story of how the city was raped has been twisted around a bit to make a proto-Christian saint out of Titus, who really didn't want to be mean to the Jews. He may have been one of the relatively good guys among emperors but there is no dodging the fact that in history he destroyed Jerusalem and its temple with efficient brutality.

But the tapestries are gentle wonderworks of another time and with another attitude. They show the emperor tricked into the destruction of the city by various evil-minded characters. The designs woven into the material are full of marvelous detail of flora and fauna that would be hard to better in a painting. Because of the evanescence of the natural dies used on the yarns, these works of art are kept in darkened rooms and only illuminated when there is someone actually there to look at them. We arrived late in the day, a few minutes before nominal closing time, but the custodian insisted in keeping the charming little place open until we had sated ourselves on the whole set. There was no admission fee and he even looked a bit awkward about accepting a few thousand lire as thanks for his kindness.

Finding a restaurant in Marsala presented some challenge because there aren't a lot of them in the center of the city. We solved the problem by stopping at the nicest *pasticceria* we came across, and asked questions after we had arranged for our ration of gin and tonic. The pastry shop was the scene of much coming and going during the *passeggiata*. Some of the people were young adults who sampled the whipped-cream goodies as well as small glasses of wine. Some were young teenagers who sat for a while and then moved on, often without buying anything at all. Lots of others had infants in their arms and, as always in Italy, admiring the *bambini* is a national delight that ranks with soccer as a spectator sport. After observing the busy life of the bar for an hour we sought advice and found the almost deserted Trattoria Garibaldi, where we had a perfectly pleasant dinner in nearly solitary splendor. The host provided an elaborate buffet of antipasto while he cooked a sauce from start to finish from fresh tomatoes and basil. The pasta was very much *al dente* and the dish worth waiting for.

Marsala turned out to have much to offer which, like the lush and ancient *arazzi* in the museum, did not become visible until we had looked around for a bit. Inspecting posters on public wall spaces, we discovered a five o'clock piano recital at a pretty little Baroque church that had been converted into a location for chamber concerts. At least the poster *said* five o'clock. Arriving a few minutes early for the free entertainment, we amused ourselves by watching the small audience assemble and listen to the piano tuner perform at great length. Lots of old friends greeted each other. The preliminaries went on for about forty-five minutes until the artist emerged in full tailcoat and regalia, ready to begin. At that point a scholarly gentleman with a clear voice and a sheaf of notes arose from the front row to deliver a fifteen-minute lecture on the development of Schubert's *oeuvre* during the middle years of his career. The music finally began around six and was well performed, if not quite world class, which is perhaps just as well since we lost the program, and the name of the artist escapes me. He is perhaps best remembered as a happy interlude of unscheduled entertainment which Marsala presented to us without fee, a pleasant and characteristic example of Sicilian generosity.

We had arrived in Marsala on a Saturday afternoon, and after having spent Sunday in the town, had been off visiting Erice on Monday. Thus it wasn't until our final day that we really saw the neighborhood of the Hotel President fully turned on and running. As in nearly all Italian cities, the vicinity that appeared drab and deserted was colorful, full of people and lively in the mornings of the weekdays. Open-air flower and vegetable stands appeared in what had been graveled open spaces near gas stations. The local bar set out a fresh array of *cornetti* and other pastry for the breakfast trade. The neighborhood *edicole* hung out a huge variety of magazines and newspapers, and even the gloomy recesses of the hardware store turned on a few lights to show off their locks, motor scooter parts, helmets and bicycles. If you want to know an Italian town, don't judge it by the state of affairs on the weekend, or *ever* between noon and 3:30 pm when all the world is home for a nap. Life will return by five when the *passeggiata* gets underway. We had seen very little sign of the famous wine trade while in Marsala. Adventurous English merchants seem to have invented this wine in the late eighteenth century by adding a good measure of brandy as a means of preserving the sweet Sicilian wines while they made the long delivery route from the Mediterranean to Bristol by ship. This followed the earlier pattern of Sherry, the wine of Xerez in Spain, which had been popular in London since Elizabethan times. Still on exhibit at the Florio winery (a part of the Cinzano conglomerate which bought up the English bottlers in the 1930s) is a letter from Lord Nelson, who ordered thousands of bottles for his officer's mess* when he came back from the Battle of the Nile in the war against Napoleon. English interest in the wine trade is credited with the presence of two British gunboats which escorted Garibaldi to his successful landing in Marsala when he began his southern sweep of the *Risorgimento* with his "thousand" red shirts in 1860. Like most Americans, I was only familiar with Marsala as flavor in a sauce for veal, so I resolved to continue my

---

*No one could drink the water on shipboard straight in the eighteenth century; it was generally too foul by the time the ship was out of port for a few weeks. The enlisted men were given a tot of rum to disinfect it and give it a more palatable taste. The officers drank wine. An unspoilable wine, one that, like Marsala, was fortified with brandy, was a godsend.

gastronomic education by ordering a short one, *"un piccolissimo bicchiere,"* as a sort of postprandial salute to this pleasant town. I was well habituated by the time we left Sicily. Try it, you'll like it!

Cathy amid the fallen drums of the gigantic columns of Temple "G" at Selinunte.

V.

SELINUNTE

The road running east along the lower coast of Sicily, the SS115, is not listed as an expressway and has only two lanes. But the lanes are wide, the visibility good, and the Italian style of passing slower-moving traffic by driving swiftly down the yellow center stripe while flashing lights on and off made for rapid progress to the east. We soon reached Mazara del Vallo, one of the major Sicilian fishing ports. We did not stop; an error in retrospect, since really every Italian town has its own charm of people, market piazza or church.*
We later learned that Mazara has a cathedral with Gagini sculptures, a pretty waterfront, a Norman castle and a Tunisian district where couscous ranks well ahead of the pasta. It

---

*The inevitable regret of anyone's first visit to Sicily, or to any country rich in history and art, is having attempted to see too many places too swiftly. This country deserves to be savored slowly: there is so much to see. Not all of it may be world-class art or even remembrable history, but much of it is, and there is interest and charm at every turn, not least in the gracious and friendly people who respond most kindly to even the most primitive attempt of a tourist to speak their language.

is the town where Count Roger de Hauteville, brother of the Guiscard, held the first Norman parliament in Sicily in 1097.

The first few signs directing us to Selinunte appeared less than an hour after leaving the Hotel Presidente in Marsala. Our route was a connector just north of a series of beach towns, each with its own access road leading south from highway 115. We pressed on and eventually took a small secondary road that indicated it went to Marinella di Selinunte. This little beach town doesn't get much of a boost from the guidebooks but it is probably possessed of a bunch of places to eat that we had neglected. There are, however, many pretty views of the sea and the neighboring ruins. Just sitting in the sun on a piece of 2,500-year-old building stone is an experience to recall.

Selinunte is one of the most extensive archeological sites in all of Italy, but arrangements for visiting it, although grandly begun, have a long way to go to completion. There are two groups of temples: the Acropolis Temples to the west, and what are known as the "East Group," nearer our point of arrival. There are at least seven temples still recognizable today. Their profusion and size give plenty of evidence that this was one of the major cities of the Greek colonies. It has been destroyed so utterly that no one today can really figure out which god was worshipped at which temple. They are known only by the letters of the alphabet. Without exception, the walls, rows of columns and architraves we can see here are all the work of more or less careful restoration in the past century and a half, some of it crude but some skillful, such as the almost complete reconstruction of Temple E in the East Group, which is accurate and impressive in size. Reassembling the scattered drums of Doric columns is fairly straightforward work, and a lot of the pieces of the entablatures and capitals go together like a three-dimensional jigsaw puzzle. But the attempts at reconstruction only made us wonder the more how this spectacular destruction and dispersal came to be. It almost appears the result of some primordial curse that not a stone should be left upon a stone in the unhappy city.

Selinunte was established nearly three thousand years ago where a little river comes down to the sea and formed a marshy harbor. Its name comes from the wild celery or *selinous* that grew there then and can still be found in the area today. The town was founded by colonists from Megara Hyblea, an eighth-century city just north of Siracusa that was later utterly destroyed by its more famous neighbor. After a couple of hundred years Selinunte was at a crest of prosperity. The array of temples really outdoes anything this side of Athens, and some of them are larger than the models of the mother country. Temple G in the East Group stands on a stylobate (the basic platform of stone pavement) that is more than 325 feet long and 160 feet wide. That is slightly larger than a soccer field. The roofed area of the temple (if it was ever completed) would have been only slightly smaller. There are remains of only two other temples of this scale in the Mediterranean circuit, one at Agrigento a few miles down the coast, and the other at Olympia in Greece. But today the great temple is a heap of huge cut and broken stones, drums of columns, capitals and fragments of frieze and cornice, fallen and jumbled in a confusion that makes it impossible to really see how they could have ever fit together. The greatest of the gigantic column drums are more than ten feet in diameter and weigh better than a hundred tons apiece. About ten miles away, in the midst of olive, orange and grape plantations are the Cave de Cusa, the quarries from which these huge stones were taken in the first place. Half-quarried pieces destined for one of the temples are still in place, abandoned when the city met its end.

Selinunte is one of those tragic, wasted remnants of an industrious people's domain that gives witness to human fury, greed, envy, blame and hostility as well as seismic bad luck. For reasons that today are either unknown or at best would seem foolish or fruitless, this city and Segesta had developed a strong mutual antipathy. Probably they were in economic competition or quarrelling about trading rights. Who knows? Does it matter? If it had not been caused by such righteous rage, it would have been for some other cause. Minor wars led to alliances with greater powers, and Segesta became an ally of Carthage, while Selinunte sought help of both Agrigento and Siracusa. Henceforth all were bound to honor pledges of mutual protection in the almost inevitable advent of war. When it happened, the ever-crafty Carthaginians moved rapidly and secretly at the behest of Segesta. Led by an early Hannibal (almost two centuries before the one who made the Alpine elephant trek) they took the town so quickly that the allies from the east had no time to arrive for its defense. Selinunte was sacked and pretty much destroyed. An attempt to rebuild met the same fate a few centuries later. The few standing temples suffered from repeated earthquakes until there was virtually nothing left to see by the later Middle Ages. The deserted strip of coastland was little visited until the sixteenth century, and real uncovering of the site, or even knowledge of the city itself, did not come about until the early nineteenth century, when the British took an archeological interest in it. Picking our way around the fallen blocks we scared up a few small chameleons that now inhabit the place. Edward Fitzgerald's lines translating Omar Khayyám's medieval Persian quatrains kept coming back to my mind even if the gods and heroes were from a different pantheon:

> *They say the lion and the lizard keep*
> *The courts where Jamshyd gloried and drank*
> *deep,*
> *And Baram, that great hunter, the wild ass*
> *Stamps o'er his head but cannot wake his sleep.*

We saw no lions, and only domesticated donkeys, but we found just as great a useless void of human accomplishment. All those people, all that planning and all that striving to what end? Today even the few attempts to put those desolate, huge, heaped-up stones together again seem a merely mercantile activity, even if the results are pleasant to look upon.

The best standing stones at Selinunte are in the restoration of Temple E near the entrance to the area. Some of the metope sculptures that have been taken away to the Archeological Museum in Palermo would seem to suggest that this monument was quite probably raised to honor Hera, whom the Romans later knew as Juno, wife and sister of Zeus. She was the daughter of Chronos, the very child of time itself, but her cult was most important because she looked after modest and married women and was the patron of childbearing. Her temple is a lovely golden structure and seems so appropriately placed that I can forgive the restorers of the past century if they have taken some liberties with the stones they found lying about. It surely *looks* as though it has been there since the early fifth century before Christ, even though the scholars tell us that at the time of the great destruction it really didn't look quite the way it does now.

What are we to think of such laying of waste? Surely it was no worse than the bombing of Coventry and Dresden. It was not on the scale of Hiroshima, Nagasaki or the fire-bombing of London. But all those cities have been rebuilt by energetic and optimistic descendants of the conquered or the conquerors. So has Rome itself. The melancholy fact is that Selinunte and the destructive rival which caused its downfall are today deserted except for scholars, archeological excavators, and picnicking tourists trying to recognize or imagine what once was here.

This attractive ruin, known as the temple of Castor and Pollux at Agrigento, is actually an assembly of pieces of a temple raised to an unknown god. It was cobbled together in the eighteenth century to please the growing tourist trade at the Valley of the Temples.

VI.

SCIACCA TO AGRIGENTO

We did not spend the night in Selinunte.
The little beach town didn't offer a lot in the way of accommodation at the end of March, and a long morning in the ruins hadn't been interrupted by a real lunch. We pressed eastward looking for the sign of a *pizzeria-ristorante*. None looked really promising for the first ten miles, but then we arrived in the shorefront town of Sciacca, perched on a cliff above a nice harbor enclosed by a manmade mole, a great stone jetty that protected moored yachts and the fishing boats returning with the morning's catch. From the distance below our vantage point in the piazza, the seawall looked as though it might contain the remains of a couple of middle-sized temples of the fourth century B.C.

For some reason—my guess is that it's the angle of reflection of the sky—the Mediterranean always looks most blue when seen from above. In places like Cinque Terre, Positano, Capri and Sorrento, the color is at its strongest. The low shores like Salerno in the south and Venice on the Adriatic give back grey, green and golden hues. Here at Sciacca, a hundred or more feet above the waterfront, the color at high noon is spectacular. Appropriately enough, the artists' pigment that gets nearest to it is called "Ultramarine Blue."

Blue paint has an interesting history in Italy and all of the art world. Before the invention of aniline dyes in the late nineteenth century, all the naturally derived blue pigments would fade, most notably Prussian Blue, which turns grey in a few years' time. The single exception in the great *Quattrocento* period of Italian painting was finely ground lapis lazuli, very expensive then and still a semi-precious mineral today. This "Permanent Blue" cost so much that artists used as little of it as possible, and contracts for many paintings commissioned at the time specified how many square centimeters (or perhaps *pollici quadri?*★) were to appear blue in the finished work. Money bespoke honor, and thus grew up the tradition that the Virgin Mary is almost invariably clothed in a blue mantle. Looking about in galleries and churches you may occasionally find that the wife of a religious painting's donor wears blue. You can surmise that this choice was a function of wealth long before it became an emulation of the Queen of Heaven.

Let's Go Italy, our favorite guide to pleasures of modest cost, recommended the Ristorante Miramare on the piazza as a place with a good tourist menu for around 20,000 lire.

★Square inches are square thumbs in Italian.

We really only wanted a sandwich and a glass of wine, but we entered the slightly formal dining room to see what simple fare was available. The *proprietario* was charming but firm. He made no *tramezzini,* no *panini gravidi* (pregnant buns), but he suggested that we order his *antipasto misto* with bread and butter. The result, he assured us, would be nutritionally the same but gastronomically much better. We generally follow the advice of hotel and innkeepers and have rarely been led wrong. Outside of the heavily travelled tourist districts of Rome, Italian restaurateurs value their reputation and self-respect much too highly to squander it by disposing of left-overs on unsuspecting visitors.

He was, of course, quite right. We were served sliced ripe tomatoes, olives both green and black, roasted red peppers, anchovies, a scattering of other vegetables, two or three different hard cheeses, and fresh mozzarella with wonderful crusty fresh bread and more butter than we could manage. His *vino bianco della casa* was light and fresh with a slight bead to it, perhaps a *Prosecco?* It was a splendid lunch in a picturebook location and cost less than 10,000 lire ($6) for each of us. I told him we would tell our friends. On your way to Agrigento, try stopping at the Miramare. The *piazza* above the harbor is a pleasant place, and the view to the south towards distant and invisible Libya is spectacular. On this near north bank of the Mediterranean the sea is ornamented both with yachts and with fishing boats. The harvest of the sea is great here and the advent of rapacious techniques for separating the fish from the water do not seem to have depleted the stocks of tuna and swordfish yet. Next to us in the uncrowded restaurant we observed a young man in immaculate white trousers and tennis sweater being served a huge risotto, which he followed with a well-piled plate of *frutti di mare* that contained calamari, mussels, shrimp and a variety of different-sized clams. In between courses he took calls on his cellular telephone. He spoke in incomprehensibly rapid Italian with some passion, all the while gesturing with his free hand to make his meaning more clear to his invisible correspondent. Hand language is such a meaningful part of Italian that I find I use it when asking my wife for help with an unrecollected verb form.

Nowhere is the change in civilization and style of life between classical and medieval times more clearly shown than in the three areas of Agrigento. The ruins and wonderful standing temples of the original city are now some miles inland from Porto Empedocle. The Greeks called the town Akragas. It flourished almost a thousand years before the empire of the Caesars and was alternately sacked and rebuilt by fellow Greeks, Romans, Byzantines and Arabs up to the desperate dark-age days when the inhabitants retreated up the neighboring hill—the ancient acropolis of refuge—where the little modern city still sprawls around the upper slopes. The Normans, French and Spanish came in their turn. Finally, when somewhat unwillingly annexed to the newly unified Italy under the house of Savoy, the modern town began to grow up. The rail transportation from the late nineteenth century winds its way around from the north slopes of the mountain, out of sight of both sea and temple. Midway between the modern buildings that have taken over the medieval town and the sea to the south is the "Valley of the Temples." The area is really a flat-topped ridge between a ravine and the coastal plain, but the temples are there, sure enough. There are as many standing, well-preserved temples here as at any place outside Greece itself, save at the magical Paestum in Campania. Five main buildings are observable. The Tempio della Concordia is the best preserved, dating from the fifth century B.C. and saved by its rededication as a Christian church when it was eight hundred years old. Fanatic Christian distaste for the pagan gods and the recurring *terremoti* of Sicily have reduced the rest to ruins. Some have been partially restored.

We drove past the archeological area and up a series of elbow turns to the modern city in the medieval location. Most of the buildings appeared new, six or seven stories high, finished outside with lots of balconies and stuccoed walls of pink, yellow and pale green. We had called ahead to reserve at the Hotel Belvedere, which we were able to find after a few circuits of asking directions, to which the inevitable and inaccurate response was, *"Sempre diritto!"*… "Straight ahead!" The hotel was aptly named, and from our room we could see the Mediterranean and the ancient temples far below. The furniture was large, darkly varnished and reminiscent of old Manhattan-rectory style interior decoration.

Walking out to discover the town later, we found the high street decorated with lattice arches that bore garlands of unlighted electric bulbs. After a bit of reflection we figured out that they had been put up for *Carnevale,* the farewell to meat that in olden days was supposed to set in after Shrove Tuesday and continue until Easter, still another week away. The thrifty town fathers had merely switched off the lights for Lent and were ready to illuminate Agrigento with a snap of the switch for the magic moment on Holy Saturday night at the mass of the Pascal Vigil. Thus *La Pasqua* would be welcomed with a brilliance that would equal the rowdy party that had preceded the season of repentance.

A pleasant little green park named for Aldo Moro, the terrorist-slain Prime Minister, marked the beginning of the main thoroughfare, Via Aetena, which rises towards the western end of the town, and is lined with attractive shops. We were looking for a comfortable sit-down bar or a nice *pasticceria.* Side streets leading sharply up steep hills seemed to direct us toward several *ristoranti,* but the climbing looked daunting. One of these streets was actually a two-block-long flight of stone steps. Eventually, after considerable window shopping, we found an appropriate rest stop and tried our usual method of questioning patron and proprietor about a good place to have dinner. The assistant bartender was a chubby twelve-year-old who obviously took great pride in helping Papà in running the establishment. We wondered at the American compulsion to be sure every child gets a shot at a college education so that he can outdo his father's profession. Here was one that was obviously happy to follow the set pattern of the home and inherit a prosperous business in the fullness of time. He had already acquired a great deal of the pride and grace that so characterizes Italian waiters and their employers. We accepted instructions on finding the Ambasciata di Sicilia.

By this time the *passeggiata* was running full bore up Via Aetena. We were grateful to dodge the stream of bodies by ducking into a little church, where a dozen nuns of assorted ages were singing hymns and bits of Gregorian chant to the accompaniment of a very small, foot-pumped organ. The little church was decorated with paintings of a teenaged girl, who was depicted as being in song herself. I braved the hushed and holy atmosphere to ask an elderly nun sitting in the rear row of chairs to help me identify *"La santa ragazza,"* the holy girl, to whom the church was dedicated. She told me it was Saint Rosalia, patroness of Sicily,* and asked if we would like to stay for mass; the Bishop would be coming in another half hour to celebrate mass for the sisters. I thanked her but we did not stay.

As we came out of the church in the gathering darkness,

---

*Santa Rosalia was a native of Palermo who died around 1160. The niece of King William II of Sicily, she was carried by angels to an inaccessible cave, where she lived for many years as a hermit on Monte Pellegrino, which rises above the town. She is said to have worn away part of the rock with her knees in her constant devotions. If anyone doubts the credibility of this statement, he or she is shown an extant depression in the stone. A chapel with a marble statue to commemorate the event has been built on the site. In Christian art Rosalia is depicted in her cave with a cross and a skull, or in the act of receiving a chaplet of roses from the Virgin. A common Sicilian expression for perseverance is to say someone has the knees of Santa Rosalia.

our attention was caught by the lighted shop windows across the street. One was a lingerie shop that displayed lavish confections of sexy underwear, mostly in shades of bridal white and cream lace. The manikins had perfect bodies and innocent expressions that were the equivalent of the statue of Santa Rosalia across the street. Next door was a religious bookstore that had thousands of pious titles on the shelves and on display in the window. The establishments, devoted to different sorts of feminine perfection, obviously cohabited this street in peace.

Our brief ecclesiastical diversion gave us a good appetite for dinner and we were happy to find it at the Ambasciatta di Sicilia, precisely where it was described to be, just down a little street appended to the south side of Via Aetena. We took the advice of the smiling waiter and ordered the Vitella e Fusilli al Pesto Siciliana. The veal was wonderfully lemony and the pasta was enhanced by a rich red sauce with lots of mysterious herbs. We later learned that the pesto came originally from Liguria. We had a bottle of an unknown Sicilian wine that suited the dinner admirably, and shared a toast to poor Rosalia who ate so little but has brought so much comfort to the hungry and the disappointed in subsequent years. We had stayed away from the wicked Italian *gelato* to this point, but when the *cameriere* suggested their own almond ice cream in a reverent tone, we were moved to order one dish with two spoons. The proprietor entered into the spirit of the thing and brought us two little glasses of almond wine *"per dopo dolce,"* on the house.

Someone has said that Italian ice cream (perhaps all ice cream) goes back to the emperor Nero who, besides being hard on Christians, and generally sick with cruelty, sent swift runners to the Apennine mountains to bring down snow that was made into imperial desserts. I would prefer a legend of a sweeter sort, perhaps something involving the spare-time activities of Santa Rosalia's transporting angels. In any case there is something heavenly about Sicilian gelato and cassata.

The upper town of Agrigento is like many other small cities in Sicily; gentle, simple, unpretentious and blessed with good food and pious faith. Unlike the deserted husk of Selinunte, around 60,000 people live here now, probably about a quarter of the number that inhabited Akragas in its most successful period around 400 B.C. Its people seem to pre-serve attitudes of the intervening centuries while availing themselves of all the trinkets and improvements of this later time. Cars and *motorini*, like the Vespa, are hugely important symbols of masculine maturity and success, but many young professional women now drive them too. Boys who haven't achieved wheels are seldom without a soccer ball. Girls are much in evidence during the evening *passeggiatta*, usually in groups of three, which leaves two to carry on together if one is successful in being picked up, quite by chance, by a young man. A considerable amount of *gelato* is consumed in these afternoon rituals, although it seems to do no damage to the figures of the *ragazze*. The direct approach of youthful affin-ity in Italy is beguiling. Grafitti, while deplorable in any city, seem more forgivable when the messages on walls read, *"Maria*

Ti AMO" or *"Marcello e Teresa"* followed by a string of hearts. In one town I found a pair of inscriptions reading *"Ti amo Ursula"* and *"Ti amo Sabrina,"* which looked suspiciously like examples of a single handwriting.

Older women often wear black in Sicily, but among the younger ones the unattached can be distinguished from the young married by skirt length. As soon as a Sicilian girl has a stable relationship with her *fidanzato,* her mini descends almost to the knee. It is a little like the location of the hibiscus blossoms behind the ears of the Polynesian girls: right ear, the girl is taken; left ear, she's available. Unlike an engagement ring, skirt length is recognizable from a distance, and is a much more flexible symbol. If a girl breaks up with her boyfriend she can always pull the *minigonna* out of the dresser drawer and return to the *passeggiata* the following afternoon.

Life in the old area below the modern city of Agrigento, on the other hand, is a far more serious business. On a good day, a thousand or more visitors come to walk through the ruins of this 2,400-year-old city, which was so much larger than its successor on the hill. After the single shock of beauty at Segesta and the melancholy waste of vast Selinunte, ancient Akragas, for all the similarity of its ruins, presents a different face. To begin with there are more people over here. Buses arrive through the morning hours, and groups with lecturing guides in a variety of languages start off from the parking lot with looks of determination and fulfillment on their faces. Thinking that the throng might clear a bit if we gave them some time, we went back to start with the museum that we had passed on the way in to the "Valley of the Temples." This city had grown up after Gela, to the east, was already flourishing in the sixth century B.C. Within a hundred years its power and strength had increased to the point that it defeated a large Carthaginian army at Himera on the north coast of Sicily. The North Africans, however, were back in force in another hundred years and took the city after a long siege. It recovered a century later and became a prize to be contended for when the Romans and Carthaginians came into their deadly conflict during the third century. As we know, Rome won, if only for a time. But epochs of five hundred or six hundred years do pass, as did the empire of the Caesars. The Byzantines came and eventually gave way to the raw new power of Islam, who called the town "Girgenti." A quarter-millennium later the Normans descended from northern Europe, eventually to breed a dynasty with the Swabian Germans. Agrigento (to use the modern form of the town name introduced by Mussolini in 1927) stayed deserted and isolated downslope from its hilltop survivor through the time of the Angevin and Spanish rulers who governed by remote control from other parts of Europe. Under the Aragonese it earned a customs freedom, which spurred some prosperity. Annexation to the newly unified Italy came hundreds of years later, in the late nineteenth century. Luigi Pirandello lived and wrote his dramas here earlier in the twentieth century.

But it is classical Agrigento that attracts visitors today. There was a scattering of tourists from many countries in the Archeological Museum, looking at bits and pieces of fifth-century temples. Most notable of these fragments is an enormous telamon, a figure of a colossal man built up of large blocks of stone, presented as standing with arms crossed back of his head, intended to serve as a support of the interior entablature of the Temple of the Olympian Zeus. The telamon, about thirty-five feet high, was designed to stand on a pedestal half the height of the temple columns. Simple addition assumes a temple of enormous proportion to include such a set of monsters; the capitals of the columns must have been around seventy feet above the temple floor. I checked the guidebook and discovered that the original building—alas, an often-quarried source of building material of the medieval period—was originally almost 370 feet long by 180 feet wide. The reassembled telamon stood on a lower floor in the museum and reared up past the balcony of a two-storey room. I tried to photograph it and asked a quartet of students if they would pose at its feet. They turned out to be Japanese and didn't do much English. We finally worked it out that I should take pictures of them with *their* cameras and then take one of my own.

The real queen of the ruins of Sicily is the Temple of Concordia here. It might have originally been dedicated to Castor and Pollux, and possibly was erected by Theron of Akragas in the fifth century. This jewel is the best preserved of all the Sicilian marvels, a happy circumstance we owe to the occasional conversions of the late Roman period. The temple was made into a Christian church by opening up the *cella* (the interior enclosure) by cutting arched openings in the side walls to light a sanctuary for the celebration of the Byzantine liturgy. It is a very impressive place, but the large crowds of Agrigento have made it necessary to shield the interior from the traffic and we were not permitted to venture inside. The Concordia temple is a classic of the hexastyle facade (six columns wide). There are thirty-four columns altogether. The dimensions of the building seem to point to the Temple of Theseus in Athens as its model. I don't know how it got the name of Concordia, but there is a local tradition that bride and groom should visit it on their wedding day to avoid a married life of perpetual controversy.

Walking about a two-thousand-year-old site gets to be a tiring and dusty business, even in late March. There are parts of at least seven temples to be seen. We kept running into the same groups of tourists and eventually helped translate a little simple Italian for a German professor of literature and his wife. The exchange was courtly and formal (in English) and cards were exchanged by the men. The pleasant socializing in the sunshine went on while we strolled up the rising path towards the temple of Juno Lacinia, which still retains about half of its original set of Doric columns. The pronounced entasis of these stone and stucco monoliths reminded me of the shape of the columns at Paestum, south of Salerno, which we had seen on a previous trip. And uphill, beyond the stubs of stone supports and occasional capital and pediment, are the cheerful and colorful stuccoes of the modern apartment houses and an occasional dome or spire of the churches of the Agrigento of today.

There is a charm to upper Agrigento. It epitomizes that combination of dark-age superstition and contemporary fashion design, rosaries and Vespas, Francis of Assisi and Federico Fellini, that visitors find in pleasant if illogical combination all over Italy. But down in the valley there is a subtler, keenly intellectual side to the background of this town that is far older, more brilliant, and just as loony as anything in *La Dolce Vita*. Here Empedocles learned and taught in the latter half of the fifth century before Christ. He learned from the disciples of the recently deceased Pythagoras and sought universal principles for his own brilliant philosophical system. He concluded that there is only one sort of change, that of motion, and only four essences of matter: fire, air, earth and water. Their rearrangement, he taught, accounts for all the diversity of nature. The Acagran people tried to make him king for some reason I cannot discover, but he refused the honor. It is said that when he grew old he tried to make a case for his total assumption into Olympian space by having his body disappear from this earth. To this end he jumped into the crater of Etna. Milton puts him in hell in *Paradise Lost*, calling him

He who to be deemed a god, leaped fondly into Etna flames...

Unfortunately, the volcano spat back one of his metal sandals in its next eruption and gave the fraud away. But Empedocles' four elements remained basic science for the next two thousand years.

VII.

AN EMPEROR & SUBSEQUENT
TRAGEDIES OF SICILIAN HISTORY

Driving through Sicily we continually confronted land-
scapes raised by an ancient geology and eroded by time and
the mismanagement of men. Like its history, Sicilian geogra-
phy presents a mixture of melancholy and beauty. In spite of
centuries of abuse, the country still produces grapes, olives
and citrus fruits in plenty, though the wheat farming of the
Roman era is largely gone. As we followed the modern highway (the 115) to the southeast, we crossed some spectacular
ravines on a roadway elevated along files of concrete pylons,
which supported the spans bridging the distance from one
ridge to the next. Some bridges were equipped with signs
warning of wind gusts, and a few had wind socks on flagstaffs
to alert us to the direction and force of the gusts. I wondered
for awhile why the Italian engineers chose to exalt the road
above the valley rather than to make low every mountain
and hill, in the more usual American style. Cheaper to build
concrete causeways than to blast away all that rock? I eventu-

ally concluded that since most American towns and cities are in valleys and many of the oldest Italian ones are on hilltops, it is simply a matter of staying at the most economical elevation for the purpose of the road. Since the long sections of prestressed concrete bridgework are supported by widely spaced columns, the final result probably does much less violence to the natural drainage and contours of the land. But then, there are occasional earthquakes to consider.

In 1693 there was a whopper of a *terremoto* that leveled whole sections of cities in the southeastern quarter of the country. Half of Ragusa, almost all of Noto and Avola, much of Modica, some of Siracusa and a score of small villages collapsed into heaps of stones. There was wealth concentrated in the aristocratic families of the Spanish counts who ruled under the haphazard supervision of the viceroys of the Bourbon kings of Spain in those days. Thus most of these communities were rebuilt, or at least the churches and homes of the rich were rebuilt, in the extreme Baroque or Rococo style of the early sixteenth century. This ushered in a time of opportunity for Vincenzo Sinatra and the other great Baroque architects. The houses of the peasants, on the other hand, were simple to begin with, the country peasants sometimes living in rubble-walled lean-to shelters. Passing through this pleasant, rolling countryside we saw a number of these roofless stone huts. It is hard to figure out if they were sheds or habitations, but being too small for garner or animal stall, I suspect they are the remains of the dwellings of the poor of previous centuries. Since the days of the *latifondie*, the large

farms owned by absentee proprietors, the workers have lived
in the villages and have walked to field or vineyard, often a
comparatively long distance away, for the day's work. I wondered about the varying economic condition of the people
of Sicily over the times we had learned about. Homer refers
to the island as a source of slaves. We don't know much about
the cost of living in rural parts of the late Roman Empire, but
to judge from the number and size of coin hordes found by
archaeologists, it was a money economy in classical times.
Under the Romans, Sicily was perhaps less based on a slave
labor than was Rome itself. Landlords from the capital held
great estates and owned slaves, but much of the island was
farmed in small patches even when wheat was being shipped
to mainland Italy in competition with or substitution for the
vast granary of Egypt. By Arabic times a sort of feudal land
tenure made for subsistence agriculture and sharecropping
that continued on into the Norman period. But the interior
of the island lacked cities, and the Norman baronage began
to choose not to live on their own land. This trend was ac-
centuated under the Angevin French and Aragonese Spanish
occupation in the thirteenth and fourteenth centuries, because of the series of tax loopholes that exempted the clergy,
appointees of the crown and, most significantly, residents of
Palermo from paying any taxes at all. The avenues of the capital
city were soon lined with *palazzi* large and small, belonging
to landowners of the surrounding countryside who had trans-
ferred their formal place of residence to the tax-sheltered
city.

Living in close proximity to each other made for a certain amount of competition in strutting about town and in the gorgeousness of the livery in which one clothed one's servants. Laws were eventually passed limiting the number of horses drawing a coach to four for the nobility and two for the untitled bourgeoisie (of which there were few anyway), allowing only the viceroy to be drawn about by six. Peasants were limited to mules and were not allowed to use saddles. Overseers in the hinterlands rode horses in the style of the Spanish *gaucho,* but the people who produced the food came down to market with their wheat in bags slung over the backs of their mules. Their crop was only a share of what they produced, and the overseer took his cut too. Not being Palermitani, they were stopped at the city gates and required to pay a considerable tax on their produce before they were able to sell it inside the city. Under the huge inequality of this kind of system of distribution of wealth, a considerable amount of brigandage developed in the countryside. The viceroy's authority didn't extend much beyond the city walls. Strong men who controlled a patch of the interior were far better guarantors of rough and ready justice than the officers and justiciars of the crown, and the poor turned to them for help and protection. Thus the sociological base of the Sicilian Mafia was laid down in the lifestyle of the country long before the institutionalized crime families grew up in later centuries. In the meantime, innumerable aristocrats and petty baronial landowners built personal palaces in towns, but no roads for commerce were built in the country. For all of the seventeenth and eighteenth centuries, the principal expense of the aristocracy was on the show and display of opulence necessary to maintain their public profile. There was virtually no investment or improvement in agricultural method for hundreds of years, while capital was being exported to the gold-inflated markets of Spanish finery and to the jewelers of Amsterdam. Not until the dictatorship of Garibaldi's provisional republic (on the way to the completion of unification in the later nineteenth century) did something in the way of land redistribution begin to come about. But even then, Sicily still lacked the infrastructure of bridges, roads and port facilities that were so common in northern Europe. Public water supply, which had been the hallmark of Roman civilization, was almost unknown until the time of Mussolini in the 1920s.

The fascists accomplished some improvement in the late twenties and thirties but were not really popular in Sicily, in spite of Il Duce's showy bounty in building movie theaters and post offices. He attempted to integrate the country more closely with mainland Italy by banning the use of the Sicilian language.* Schools were required to be conducted in the most formal Tuscan, and the police were supposed to speak

---

*What many Americans call "dialects" in Italy are really not debased forms of a proto-Italian language, but autonomous languages in their own right, quite as old and equally descended from Latin as the literary Tuscan dialect that was chosen as the "national language" after the *Risorgimento* had unified Italy in the 1870s. Although there was literature in the languages of Naples, Venice, Milan, the Piedmont, and especially Sicily, the world fame and undoubted excellence of the works of Boccaccio,

in the language of Dante, or at least that of Boccaccio. An odd result of this policy is that today, while all Italians who grew up since World War II speak the standard Italian of schools and TV announcers, Sicilians use a slightly more formal grammar and a less slangy approach to tenses than do Neapolitans, Romans or Florentines. Sicilians favor the historical past over the perfect and imperfect tenses and use the most polite and formal pronouns in everyday discourse. The medieval custom of being allowed, as a sign of favor, to kiss the hand of one's lord still hangs on in Sicily; bishops and *monsignori* as well as Mafiosa godfathers present their hands to be honored by a subservient and grateful faithful.

Perhaps those godfathers would no longer be present had Mussolini succeeded in his attempt to displace the Mafia before and during World War II. The Mafia fought back by becoming the most effective partisans of the interior and spies

---

Petrarch, and Dante made the selection of the Tuscan language of the thirteenth century a natural choice. Even though the king, Vittorio Emanuele, spoke Piedmontese at home, he could manage in Tuscan. It was read by the intelligentsia of the time and existed in books all over Italy, even though less than 20 percent of the population was then literate. Today a university preparatory course in an Italian secondary school includes a three-year course in Dante, one each for *Inferno, Purgatorio,* and *Paradiso.* Radio and TV announcers go to special training institutes to perfect a good Tuscan accent, of which Sienese is thought to be the most pure. Everyone can read Petrarch's sonnets with greater facility than most college-educated Americans can read Shakespeare or Milton. Nearly everyone speaks two languages: standard Italian, and a local "home dialect," which is the somewhat Italianized version of the old native tongue in which they converse around the family kitchen table, in homemaking or lovemaking, or in the authentic speech of Fellini films such as *Amarcord.* Today universities offer courses in Sicilian, a nearly lost language in which the earliest Italian literature was written at the court of Roger de Hauteville.

of the port towns. When the local bureaucrats were turned out of office after the invasion, the American military government replaced them with the most reliable anti-fascists they knew, and effectively reestablished the "men of honor" in a position of respect and power from which the present government is still trying to dislodge them.

I sometimes wonder why Cosa Nostra doesn't just turn over the page and try going straight. Given the present prosperity of all of Italy, they would probably make as much or more money and have to work fewer long and dangerous hours to accomplish it. They surely have ample capital to set up any sort of business they could choose. Although virtually invisible to tourists (who indirectly fund the protection racket of fleecing hotel keepers and restaurateurs), the Mafia still does terrible things that you read about in the newspapers when visiting Italy. On our last trip there was a great deal of outrage over a young man whose loan for his drycleaning establishment had been called in after a fire destroyed his store. After threats that the lives of his wife and child were in jeopardy if he defaulted, he committed suicide rather than turning to crime himself to raise the payments demanded by his unlicensed lender. U.S. banks make lots of money at the 20 percent interest rates many charge for credit card debt. By just cutting their rate to a competitive level, Cosa Nostra could probably make up on volume what they lost on price, and reduce their expenses by not needing to spend so much in keeping clear of the *carabinieri*.

The last great ruler of an independent Sicily was

Frederick II, who held tight control of the sunny island in the first half of the thirteenth century. I mentioned him earlier, but as the most powerful of all Sicilian leaders he deserves a little more space on his own. Frederick (surely first to give that name the extraordinary popularity it has maintained for centuries in Europe) was a German on his father's side, but a Norman Sicilian by his mother. His maternal grandfather was Roger II; his paternal grandfather was Frederick Barbarossa, the fierce, red-bearded and effective Holy Roman Emperor who was able to depose a pope and governed much of Europe, partly from the saddle and partly from his German center of power beyond the Alps. Barbarossa, the Hohenstaufen, took up the cross at the age of fifty-five and drowned crossing a river on the way to Jerusalem twelve years later, in 1190. But before this unhappy turn of events he had arranged to marry his son Henry to Constance, the daughter of Roger II of Sicily, the builder of the Palatine Chapel. The young lady was born so late in time that she arrived shortly after the death of her powerful, blond-bearded father. With the passing of time she outlasted her brother William I (who built Monreale Cathedral) and her nephew William II, known as The Good. That attractive young man was the one who had as his Queen the beautiful Joan Plantagenet, daughter of Henry II of England, and sister to Richard the Lionhearted. He seemed destined to carry on the dynasty.

But the untimely deaths of the beautiful young couple left the Sicilian barons the choice of allegiance to a German king (Henry VI Hohenstaufen, who was by then Holy Roman Emperor), or a quasi-legitimate Sicilian also descended from the Norman line. He bore the romantic proto-Sicilian name of Tancred, and he ruled Sicily for a number of years until William's aunt Constance, at the age of forty, produced a male heir, son of the Hohenstaufen. Her years and the adventurous life of her husband (who was off at a war most of the time) made many suspect that she might have been pregnant by another. Constance countered this canard by having a tent erected in the market square of Jesi, near Ancona in the Marches of east central Italy. There she bore the child and there she showed many witnesses that despite her age, she was able to nurse the child at her own brimming bosom. The lady's forthcoming attitude never totally quelled rumors that she might have been bedded by a demon or a butcher of the local market, but her husband had no doubt. He took arms against Tancred in order to secure Sicily for himself and his infant son. Henry won the entire island for a time, but he died of an undiagnosed illness in 1197, leaving his wife as regent for a three-year-old King of Sicily, Frederick Hohenstaufen, who was destined to grow up as the amazing "Child of Apulia," *Stupor Mundi,* the Wonder of the World, the last great emperor of Europe before Napoleon seven hundred years later.

Frederick's upbringing was certainly unique. His mother, who not a few thought might have poisoned her husband, was ten years older than his father, and prudently wrote a will making the pope, Innocent III, her son's guardian in case of her untimely death. She cordially disliked all the Germans and, when she died, the Sicilian barons and bishops took turns in "protecting" the four-year-old king in a series of political exchanges that left him quite vulnerable and without any real resource of his own. The pope ignored him. The local bishop, Walter of Palermo, seems to have been mostly out of town from Frederick's seventh year until he was twelve. The child was evidently left to wander, play and explore the marketplaces quite unsupervised. It was a romantic boyhood worthy of a tale from the contemporary Arabian Nights. Frederick had already learned to read and write well, and was obviously a quick study; he soon also learned French, Latin, Greek, Sicilian, Arabic and perhaps even some Hebrew—the languages of his future subjects. He got to know the life and practice of the Greek Orthodox, the Latin Christians and the Muslims. The real protectors of his youth seem to have been the people of Palermo, who loved him as their own. He had been born in Italy and was growing up there, ample reason for his loyal subjects to ignore his German antecedents. Pope Innocent may have deprived him of the "Kingdom of Rome" (to which he had been elected quite legitimately while in the cradle), and the Swabians ignored his possible claim to inherit his father's realm as Holy Roman Emperor north of the mountains (his uncle, Philip of Swabia took over that patrimony). But the inquiring and obviously intelligent little boy felt like a king and acted like one, despite his relative poverty and lack of courtiers or an army. The people of Palermo were his court and his tutors. After all, he was descended from the Guiscard and the Great Count Roger I as well as Roger II, the builder of the state of Sicily, the most prosperous realm in all of Europe.*

Frederick's reign seems to have been a series of long and ineffectual arguments with various popes. All told, he was excommunicated four times, usually for having failed to go crusading in spite of having promised to do so. His relationship with Palestine was enriched by his marriage to Yolande of Brienne, who brought him the title of "King of Jerusalem." When he did finally get to the Holy Land it turned out to be more of a state visit than a crusade. He and the courtly El Kamil, Sultan of Egypt, exchanged embassies and gifts that eventually resulted in a bloodless, diplomatic retaking of Jerusalem by Frederick that left the Mosque of Omar in the custody of the Moslems. He also got possession of Bethlehem and Nazareth. In Jerusalem in 1229 he crowned himself in order to spare any bishop the problem of his current excommunication. He got out from under the papal ban within a year.

Back home in Sicily, Frederick settled down to promulgating law and following his intellectual passions. He set forth a great and comprehensive code of laws (the *Liber Augustalis*), and encouraged poetry, science and the arts. His own schol-

---

*And what a place it was for the growth of the accretive and curious mind of a young king. Linguistically, historically, economically and politically, it was the crossroads of civilization. Even old Pope Innocent said of his ward's dominion, "His hereditary land, rich and noble beyond the other kingdoms of the world, is the port and navel of them all."

arship and close scientific observations were published in his huge work on hawking, *On the Art of Hunting with Birds*. This first work on ornithology really embraces the entire natural history of the species and still remains the essential work on hawks. Little has been added in the last three-quarters of a millennium to what Frederick learned and wrote about in the four volumes of this work.

Frederick was liberal in his court policies and seemed to allow all to have their own religion, except for Christian heretics, whom he persecuted quite savagely. He sought learning from scholars all over the world and had their books copied out and read to him. He kept an extensive harem in Palermo in a most unchristian fashion, but these beautiful imported women were also expected to be useful in his nascent silk industry. For all his open-mindedness, he could be cruel, both in serving out justice and experimenting on human beings. He had a group of babies brought up by nurses who would not speak to them, in order to determine which language may have evolved first. The babies died. He had a criminal sealed up in a barrel to be able to say that his "spirit" could not have escaped to go to either heaven or hell. To study the effect of battle stress on digestion he had several men sacrificed to study their stomach contents before and after a fight.

Frederick thought of himself as God-appointed to rule the world. Given his intellectual, diplomatic, legal, scientific, administrative and artistic talents, no one of the Middle Ages could have made such a claim with as much justification.

Since Frederick's time most of Sicilian history is an account of which foreign power has been raping it most recently. After the death of *Stupor Mundi*, Pope Clement III passed the country like a hand-me-down overcoat to Duke Charles of Anjou, who had done some service to the papacy by capturing and beheading Conradin, Frederick's fifteen-year-old grandson, the last legitimate descendant of both Roger II of Sicily and Frederick Barbarossa. Charles never got to Sicily at all, but he sent tax collectors and soldiers who precipitated a great rebellion in 1282. Because it began at eventide on Easter Monday, the uprising became known as the "Sicilian Vespers." It was sparked by French soldiers handling some married women of Messina with too much familiarity.*The street riot rapidly grew into a popular revolution and seemed like the main chance for home rule. But such was not to be. Twenty years of war followed, and the island wound up in the hands of the Spanish. Through various marriages of kings and emperors in the northern part of the continent, Sicily finally was acquired by Austria after Napoleon's conquests (which had never included Sicily). Lots of duchies and princely realms were redealt like a well-shuffled

---

*Among other sexual customs introduced by the French was the *Jus Prima Noctis,* colloquially known as the "Drôit du Seigneur," whereby the feudal lord had the right to take all brides of his demesne to bed on the first night of their marriage. It was supposedly only exercised in cases of extreme beauty or when it might prevent the unfulfilled bridegroom from discovering that his bride had not come to the altar a virgin, a circumstance that could have awful consequences and was thus better attributed to the impersonal libido of the baron. In any case, the introduction of this custom did nothing to endear the French to their new subjects in Sicily.

pack of cards by Talleyrand and other players at the Congress of Vienna in 1815. The "Two Sicilies" of the island kingdom and Naples stayed with the Spanish Bourbons until the middle of the nineteenth century. Thence Cavour, Mazzini and Garibaldi, Vittorio Emanuele, Hemingway's *Farewell to Arms*, several world wars, Il Duce, the rise of international Communism, the Christian Democrats, the Vespa, Fellini movies, and the "Economic Miracle" of the past three or four decades. Italian political history in the nineteenth and early twentieth centuries is far too complex to follow in detail despite the existence of some beguiling characters like the liberal intellectual aristocrat the Principe di Belmonte. One of my favorites is Pedrocchi, who built a classically-styled *caffè* in Padua in the 1820s. He told the waiters that all university students were to be given a copy of a somewhat left-wing newspaper and a glass of water gratis. In the process he is said to have provided an intellectual foundation for a part of the *Risorgimento* as well as a headquarters for some of its participants.

Although Sicilians were the first to follow Garibaldi, they fought then to rid themselves of their Bourbon king and had little interest in submitting to the rule, however constitutional, of Vittorio Emanuele, King of Piedmont, and Conte di Cavour, his prime minister. Today, still calling themselves Sicilians rather than Italians, they have finally settled for the status of a special region within the unified Italy. Since the thirteenth century they had never had a ruler who spoke their language, the ancient tongue of poetry and song that Mussolini did his best to eradicate.

VIII.

RAGUSA

We continued on the coast road, the 115, to the southeast, once again looking for a lunch stop in an unknown countryside. We followed one of the small side roads that lead down towards the coast on our right. This one bore an attractive sign that promised an establishment called Stella del Mediterraneo, Falconara. We followed, and eventually found an inn at the end of a narrow parking lot in a beach community. Although other signs proclaimed that the restaurant was reserved for the guests of the inn, there seemed to be none of these in evidence and the gracious blonde hostess was happy to set us up for another lunch of antipasto, bread and butter, very good Gorgonzola cheese and wine. The lady spoke quite reasonable English from her school days and turned out to be born German, married to an Italian and hoping to travel someday to America so she could have breakfast at Tiffany's in New York. It almost broke my heart to explain to her that Truman Capote's heroine, Holly Golightly, was an excessively naive young lady whose success in travelling clueless through America in the 1950s was both miraculous and unrepeatable. She was genuinely sad to hear that Tiffany and Co. was not up to providing the sort of *colazione* that she could order at the Plaza a couple of blocks up the street. To judge from the bottles on the bar, the Stella del Mediterraneo had a largely German clientele, but that is true of all tourist resorts in southern Europe.★ We made note to remember it for its pretty location on the shore and pleasant accommodation.

Sightseeing after a good lunch has never been one of my strengths, and I was delighted to find that there are special pull-off areas well marked in advance along Sicilian highways where I could stop for a fifteen-minute nap before pressing on again. Thus refreshed, we followed along the 115 and wound through the small city of Gela, where we could see two large oil drilling rigs several miles offshore to the south. Sicily has provided Europe with a significant source of useful petroleum products since ancient times. The "Greek Fire" with which Roman galleys were discouraged by Archimedes was an ancestor of napalm, made from the natural mineral

---

★A true Italian bar can be recognized by the *objets d'art* you find among the bottles on the top shelf of the mirrored backdrop. Germans favor elaborately lidded steins encrusted with bright ceramic figures representing trolls, bearded singers and Rhine maidens. Italians choose devotional items such as pictures of the Madonna, a saint or two, a color television tuned to the soccer match (often a rerun), and almost inevitably a crucifix positioned so that it seems to grow upward from the space between two bottles of cordial in the top row and spreads forgiving arms above their corks or plastic stoppers. Sometimes a red vigil light twinkles in front of a painted image of the Mother of Mercy.

asphaltic ooze that came out of the ground in a number of places on the island. Today there is a bustling petroleum trade in the whole southeast, the only part of Italy to be so economically blessed and environmentally jeopardized. Gela is reputed to have an excellent archeological museum, a chaotic city government, and one of the most pervasive Mafia racket organizations in Sicily. We decided to wish them well in their hope of reform, but not to stop on this trip.

Not long before we reached Ragusa, the 115 turned inland and climbed a series of escarpments to a rolling upland of farms and fruit trees that looked prosperous but certainly not overcultivated. Thence we turned south and began to descend a gently sloping, somewhat scruffy series of neighborhoods that became slightly more urban as we went along. Before Ragusa was devastated by the 1693 earthquake, this upper part of the town was scarcely yet built upon and presented the opportunity for a new city laid out on modern lines. Accordingly, here the blocks are rectilinear and of uniform size, but unfortunately the area has none of the charm of the older sector farther down below. We had the names of a couple of possible hotels from guidebooks, but had not made a reservation, since the current "low season" paucity of tourists seemed to leave plenty of room for inspection before choice. Presently we drew alongside a somewhat modern church where a well-dressed funeral crowd was gathered, seemingly waiting for arrival of the corpus. Using my newfound skill with the polite conditional tense I questioned a man on the curb from the window of the car: "Signore, potrebbe dirmi dove posso trovare un'albergo, non troppo caro—forse tre stelle—qui vicino?"

He looked at the shiny car and took in the fact that I was wearing a snappy new bright yellow print Italian necktie, seemed to make a mental calculation as to what I meant by "not too expensive, perhaps three stars," and smiled.

"Rafael," he said, and then added as Italians seem always to do, "Sempre dritto."

So we went right ahead down the hill, which grew steeper as we approached a neighborhood of more interesting architecture. We soon descried the sign of another hotel we had seen mentioned in a guidebook. Parking off the side of the hill on the tree-lined but narrow Corso Italia, I went in only to discover that the house was *"completo; prenotato,"* already booked solid, for the members of a commercial convention. The desk man was not particularly helpful. Back on the Corso we rolled a dozen more yards down the hill and found a rather small entry labled "Rafael." We were a bit put off by the four stars under the title of what seemed a modest *albergo*.

We later learned that the fourth star had more to do with a pair of shiny new Dodge shuttle vans that the Rafael ran to the beaches as a service to their guests in the "high season" than it did with the size and quality of their accommodation. The rate for various seasons turned out to be extremely variable, £220,000 when the water was swimmable and £120,000 in spring, winter and fall. The room had a tiny interior sitting room with a fridge and modern furniture, which included a large television mounted high on the wall for bed viewing.*There were interesting prints of unknown contemporary artists' work on the walls, and in the hall there was a signed photograph of a wedding party that seemed to consist of an Italian film actress and a middle-eastern oil sheik. We had been getting used to living at the upper end of our budget, and the Rafael also said they supplied breakfast in their subsidiary *Caffè-Bar* next door. The desk in the little lobby was presided over by a very elderly lady who seemed to be the mother of the proprietor and who was inevitably watching a soccer match on TV whenever we passed through her domain. The hotel had a modern elevator which we rode to the floor above our destination so that we could then carry the bags down to our room a half-flight below. The old lady, who was supported by a substantial cane, got off the lift one flight below and climbed the half-story difference because, she explained, her *artrite* made it easier to go up stairs than down. She suggested that we stay on board for one more stop and walk back down with the luggage. The Rafael turned out to be an agreeable venue for our planned two-night stay and not too extravagant in cold weather, when the rates of the *bassa stagione* applied. The recommendation of the met-by-chance mourner at the funeral bore out the reliability of soliciting local knowledge while navigating about Sicily.

---

*Following the news and viewing advertising on Italian TV is one of the best ways of improving one's command of the language while in Italy. You already know most of the script, and the accent and pronunciation are clear and repetitive. During Holy Week we also discovered a dramatization of the reigns of Kings Saul, David, and Solomon. It is always easier to understand the language when you know how the story turns out.

Walking farther down the sloping city from our hotel we came to the escarpment that divides Ragusa from the old town of Ragusa Ibla. Serpentine streets scale the divide, but it can also be negotiated more directly by several flights of stairs right next to the church of Santa Maria delle Scale (Holy Mary of the Stairs) where the view is best. After calculating the gradient of the trip back up from the lower city, we returned to our semi-legal parking place half up on a sidewalk around the corner from the Rafael, and drove around the longer way to Ibla below.

The lower city turned out to be less studded with historic buildings than we had hoped, although there is a pretty park at the crest of the south end of the town. The great *terremoto* of 1693 obviously did great damage here as well. The churches have been rebuilt in the most enthusiastic style of the High Baroque. The Basilica di San Giorgio is a prime example. It convinced me that when you have carefully inspected one Baroque church, it begins to resemble all the rest of them in retrospect. The two great churches of San Giorgio and San Giuseppe in this town are decorated with similar orders of columns, with swirls and volutes, dental moldings and balustrades that so impress the eye that the basically different shapes of the facades were hard to remember and identify when we were sorting photographs at home. Perhaps when you've seen one, you've seen 'em all. But inside the basilica it was another matter altogether. The interior of San Giorgio was veiled according to the custom of covering all the ornamentation of the sanctuary during Lent. I had not seen this done so completely in any other church. Usually during this penitential season the elaborately sculpted and ornamented statues are covered with purple drapes to subdue the mind to penance in the weeks before Good Friday and Easter. Here the veil was an enormous canvas scrim hanging from high up in the dome, perhaps sixty feet above, reaching to the steps of the altar. The bluish cloth was painted, quite skillfully, as a huge-scale, well-drawn crucifixion that included a Roman soldier in the very moment of breaking the legs of one of the crucified thieves. The effect of this rough temporary banner in the midst of the Ionian cream-and-golden detailing of the walls was almost brutally powerful. The crossing of the church was very high, and the air very cold. Sun streamed in through the windows and from the lantern above, and we could hear the wind whistling through their missing panes.

Seeking a simple lunch, we sought counsel of an elderly lady, a postcard vendor at a *tabacchaio,* and were directed to Il Saracenù, just off the lower end of the cathedral square in Ibla. While enjoying a pizza we reflected that there were no tourists in this *trattoria.* We then realized that we saw almost no tourists in any part of Ragusa. The town prides itself on the fact that there is nothing much going on here and the place is *tranquilla e piacevole,* peaceful and pleasant. Everyone seemed glad to have us there but no one was hustling tourists for a living. Being in need of a little tranquility ourselves, we settled in and spent three nights in Ragusa.

The archeological museum of Ragusa is situated on the

lower floors of a building that up above opens onto Via Roma, and is the location of a sizable *STANDA*, a department store of the ilk of a small Wal-Mart crossed with a middle-sized supermarket. The building is perched on the edge of a deep ravine that divides the east and west sections of upper Ragusa. I couldn't find the stair leading down to the lower levels, so we took the car and parked in front of the museum, two or three levels below the Via Roma, which bridged the defile over our heads.

The museum is splendidly organized, well labeled in Italian, logically arranged and virtually devoid of visitors. We spent a pleasant hour among the artifacts of the western Syracusan colonies of the third to fifth centuries B.C. There is also a considerable exhibition of artifacts from Hybla Heraea, the city of the Siculi that had traded with Syracusan colonies in the early first millennium. Evidently the Greek and its successor Roman town were pretty much destroyed by the brief incursion of the Vandals in the fifth century. The name "Ragusa" was brought by seventh century A.D. colonists from Byzantine Dalmatia. Although its hilly location looks easily fortifiable, it fell to the Saracens in the ninth century and again to the Normans a couple of centuries later. Sicily is full of places that look impregnable, but since there is no one speaking classical Greek there today, we can be sure that through skill, strength, craft or treachery, all the fortifications eventually failed. From the French Maginot Line to Hitler's "Fortress Europe," it has taken military thinkers a very long time to grasp this inevitable reality.

Later we climbed to the higher reaches of the upper town and inspected the exterior of the *duomo* in Piazza San Giovanni. The church itself always seemed to be closed or *in restauro* whenever we were in range to visit it, but we heard mysterious organ music coming from behind the locked gates as we walked around it. There is much first-class Baroque architecture in Ragusa as well as charming sculpture of the Gagini school. We found some of it by following the instructions in the *Blue Guide*. We ended up convinced that there was much more yet to be seen than initially met the eye.

One of the best bargains for a first-class dinner was the Pizzeria-Ristorante La Valle on the Via Risorgimento, which we found on our first trip. To find it we crossed the valley it was named for on a three-hundred-foot bridge of stone arches, which looked to me to be of Roman design and construction. Since it is called the Ponte Vecchio and is limited to foot traffic I think it could well be of that age, but I could find no mention of it in any guidebook. Maybe being a mere 1,700 years old is just too recent to be worthy of note in this antique island. La Valle was a bustling place with families and businessmen dining well and being expertly served by white-jacketed waiters, who suggested well and presented each dish with a flourish. After an excellent dinner of a delicate Coteletta di Vitella alla Milanese and a broiled Petto di Pollo, I indulged my recently acquired pleasure of a *"piccolissimo bicchiere di Marsala"* as a *digestivo*. I am not quite sure what a really prime Marsala is supposed to taste like, but this one had the best balance between sweet and dry of any I tried in Sicily. Reflecting that the dinner for two with wine and such cost us about $28, we decided to try again, braving a cold March wind sweeping across the bridge on the following night. We settled in at a table next to a steam radiator and were comfortable. The climate of Sicily may be semi-tropical in summer, but *Marzo pazzo*, "Mad March," is unpredictable all over Italy. Even if you come in April, remember to bring a sweater. Ragusa is truly *piacevole e tranquila*, but there is a touch of melancholy about this town too. It sits in the middle of an area that has been civilized and populated in large and well-appointed cities for close to three thousand years. Today it supports a much smaller population in a few cities and towns at what seems a fairly modern European standard of living. But what of all those other communities? The unnamed necropoli are almost the only remnant of their existence. Grave goods brought to the archeological museums in two or three locations evidence a skillful, artistic and prosperous people in the ages of Greece, Rome, Islam, the Normans and the early days of the Spanish remote-control monarchy of the "Two Sicilies." The extravagant Baroque facades bespeak great wealth even after the terrible earthquake at the end of the seventeenth century. Now many of the churches are closed for lack of either priests or parishioners, and a number of elegant old houses seem deserted. There were many more people here in 400 B.C. or in 1400 A.D. than there ever have been since.

IX.

PIAZZA ARMERINA

We left the sloping civility of Ragusa and took the road inland toward Caltagirone, a town of 40,000 in the interior where good ceramic clays have been mined since ancient days. Tile, majolica ware and other pottery are still made here in quantity. Like most of this part of the country, Caltagirone lost its most ancient architecture to the great tremblor of 1693. It was rebuilt in a time of some prosperity and should have been a sensible lunch stop for us. But we had not calculated on the small size of Sicily or the good quality of the roads in the interior, and sped past the little city still without appetite at eleven in the morning. We thus missed seeing the famous Scala, a flight of 142 steps with colored figures in tile on their risers. The *Blue Guide* describes the design as "splendid" but the climb as "tiring," and the church at the top as "usually locked." We proceeded north without too much conflict of motive.

Coming from the south towards Piazza Armerina we went through a colorful series of well-cultivated plateaus

checkered with green and buff fields in a countryside devoid
of signboards, gas stations or other signs of twentieth-century
development. Here again the pattern of Sicilians living in
villages and travelling considerable distances each day to the
fields was repeated. Neatly lettered road signs urged us on.
And then we rounded a hill and saw a great distance
ahead where the huge blue and white shape of Etna rose
above the horizon. Later, checking on a map, I calculated that
the mountain was still 45 to 50 statute miles from where we
first glimpsed it. It seemed amazingly large. Fully one-third
of its height was covered with snow, punctuated on the lower
slopes with outcroppings of black rock. A layer of cloud hovered above the summit, but it looked like local weather rather
than a plume from the caldera. The whole, even from that
distance, looked ominous and menacing to me. Not the sort
of thing I would name an insurance company after. The Sicilians just call it "La Montagna."

Etna is immense. The great sloping cone is close to thirty
miles in diameter and the summit reaches more than two
miles above sea level. The official altitude of 10,926 feet makes
it the highest volcano in Europe, considerably higher than its
companion Vesuvius to the north. It erupts regularly, most
recently in 1978, 1979, 1986, and 1992, new lava vents breaking through the surface along the lines of old faults in the
crust. But trusting Italians have been constructing vacation
villas on its slopes at such a vigorous pace that the government has had to pass laws to keep the view-loving brave from
settling real estate right up the south side of the mountain.

Great eruptions have destroyed the greater part of Catania on the coast several times in the historical past. Any contour map shows that it is the great geographical feature of Sicily and takes up the center of the whole eastern third of the island. Sicily has about the same land area as the state of Maryland, and Etna covers a space slightly larger than the area between Washington and Baltimore. It ranks as one of the half-dozen largest volcanos in the world.

Catching occasional glimpses of the mountain as our road rose and fell in rolling countryside, we progressed towards Piazza Armerina. Our destination was Villa Romana del Casale, about a mile to the southwest of Piazza Armerina, but you have to navigate through part of the little city to get to it in its little country valley. We had heard much of this site and its famous mosaics of "bikini girls" doing their exercises. No one is quite sure who built it and commissioned the extraordinary colorful floors that are almost the only surviving evidence of what must have been an amazing pleasure palace. It is so big (3,500 square meters of pavement survive) that some scholars feel that only an emperor could have afforded its construction. Maximian is the logical candidate on the basis of date and life history. He was co-emperor (in charge of the West) with Diocletian from 296 to 305 A.D., but resigned the job and was thought to have retired to Sicily. He failed to stay out of active politics for long and, lacking an army, was forced to commit suicide as a way of ensuring a more permanent retirement from public life.

Whether it was Maximian or some other fabulously rich

Roman of the end of the third century is debatable. The only thing we know about the builder was that he had great taste in floors. A clear plastic shelter in the shape of the original house has been erected above the mosaic pavements and equipped with steel and aluminum walkways that allow the visitor a wonderful view of the floors without getting them worn out by the feet of a daily flux of hundreds of tourists. Besides the ten pretty young ladies in the bare-midriff costumes playing with beach balls and pinwheels, there are scenes of the hunt, cherubs fishing with nets in a dream harbor, a whole menagerie of deer, elk, oryx, lion and ostrich, as well as luxurious domestic scenes, such as ladies on their way to the baths with a half-dozen attendants bearing towels, soap and perfume. The house has rooms and apartments for ceremonial dining, family living, proper Roman bathing and what the map in the guidebook called the "Cubiculum of Erotic Scenes," which I was unable to locate. Gardens and fountains around about give the idea that it must have been a pleasant little palace in which to live and entertain if one had a staff of sixty or eighty to maintain the place and serve. The irony of its anonymous ownership reminds me of Shelley's *Ozymandias* and the warnings of the Book of Ecclesiastes. Archeology keeps turning up new evidence that all vanities decay in time, usually sooner rather than later. In this case, recovery by archeology was supported and encouraged by the vanity of the fascist government of the 1920s to encourage tourists to come here and help Piazza Armerina prosper.

The condition of these mosaics is quite wonderful. The building may have been inhabited by someone even into the Islamic period of the tenth and eleventh centuries, when it was quite probably destroyed by one of the Norman Williams (the Bad more likely than the Good), who did such a thorough job of pulling the building down that the trash and broken building materials protected the mosaics for eight hundred years, when they were uncovered by modern excavators. Digging and some restoration still go on today. The skill of one scholarly-looking gent fitting a few tesserae into a vacant patch of a mosaic scene made me wonder how much of which section had been restored in the half-century and more since its rediscovery.

The Duomo of Enna. This facade is from the early sixteenth century, an example of the transition from the Renaissance style to the Baroque.

X.

ENNA

As we drove north from Piazza Armerina the land rose until views in all directions became more and more extensive. In an hour of steady but gentle climbing we came in sight of the small city of Enna, capital of the province of the same name, and for centuries the only real *città* in the interior of Sicily. It was silhouetted above us, arranged along the crest of a tabletop mountain at an elevation of well over three thousand feet. It is said to be the loftiest city in Europe; I was not inclined to believe this until I realized that virtually all European cities were built in valley sites, along rivers or in proximity to natural harbors. This one was situated for safety on a nearly unscalable rock in the very center of Sicily. The road up makes a couple of hairpin turns and eventually enters a great rift that cleaves the south side of the city and provides a steeply sloping access. Another sharp angle uphill put us on the Via Roma, climbing toward the duomo and the only real hotel in Enna, Albergo Sicilia, which boasts a three-star rating and is a very comfortable accommodation, but not outrageously costly at $83 for the night considering the elaborate breakfast bar and bathroom. The facilities would do credit to a U.S. Holiday Inn, even though they lack the typical American provision of a thin plastic envelope of instant coffee on the bathroom counter. And the view is a lot better at the Sicilia.

Enna is the exact geographical and geometrical center of Sicily. On a clear day from the Lombard Tower at the east end of the town you can see the distant blue bulk of ice-clad Etna, fifty miles away, rearing three times higher into the sky. Enna is a medieval city with signs of early occupation still visible. The Torre di Federico and the Castello di Lombardia probably were both built by Frederick II*. These severe octagonal forms are characteristic of his strictly military strongholds, designed for domination and not for luxurious living. Frederick did not allow his vassals to use his war towers for homes. Only he lived in a totally secure domicile. His towered castles in Calabria and Puglia, as well as in Sicily itself, were strictly for the king's business of domination and defense.

---

*It is evidence of how old Sicily is that we cannot be precisely sure who built what, even in the case of huge constructions that obviously required a great host of workers over many years. It was, after all, so long ago.

Enna has a long history, which stretches back into mythology. This is the very place where Pluto, gloomy god of the underworld, came upon Persephone gathering lilies in the lovely hillsides around the mountain and carried her off to his shadowed kingdom of Dis to be his wife. This is usually called the "Rape of Persephone" but, like many of the rapes of classical mythology, it must have really been more of a forcible and unrefusable proposal of marriage. Their union (despite her occasional lapses into narcolepsy) has lasted for an eternity, or at least as long as the Greek legends live, so it is presumably going strong today. Even such a puritan as John Milton in writing *Paradise Lost* looked upon the event as having a touch of romance about it:

> *Proserpine gathering flowers,*
> *Herself a fairer flower, by gloomy Dis*
> *Was gathered.*

The poor thing was terrified at being carried off by an immortal god, especially by such a menacing prince of darkness. She loosed her hold on the lilies, which fell about the fields of Sicily. They became the daffodils, and thus placed all of us from northern climates in debt to the forcibly united couple for all the lovely springs of both New and old England.

In a somewhat more recent period, Gelon, the local hero of Siracusa, built a temple here dedicated to the grain goddess Demeter, Persephone's mother. The natural location made the growing city a quasi-impregnable stronghold, but Dionysius I, tyrant of Siracusa in a later age (397 B.C.) managed to take it through the treachery of some of its citizens whom he presumably slaughtered anyway. In Roman days, Enna was the scene of a slave's rebellion which held out against a two-year-siege before bowing to the inevitable blades or crucifixions of Roman discipline. It fared little better when the Saracens came in 839. They succeeded in finding an entry via a sewer through which they climbed by night to infiltrate the city. The Normans forced their way up the slope to conquer the starving garrison in 1087. It seems that Enna has always been "pregnable" by the determined and the patient. Today you can drive right up and enjoy the views in all directions. When we arrived, the matching but smaller and more medieval hill town of Calascibetta was a wonder of golden stone and purple *chiaroscuro* in the afternoon sun. Later, from the pleasant park at the east end of the little city, we again caught a glimpse of Etna high on the eastern horizon.

Such long-distance beauty can be ephemeral from the height of Enna. Perfectly ordinary cumulus clouds drifting across Sicily in the prevailing westerly wind often do not rise above the city. Suddenly bright blue sky and sunshine turns to a pea-soup fog that almost obscures the other side of the street. The temperature drops and the Ennans nod wisely and say that "La Paesana è arrivata." Paesana might be translatable as a female companion of one's native countryside; in Enna it is a local term for the chilly mist that arrives in the midst of fair weather. We did find Enna cold in late March.

One of the pleasures of being in each new Italian town is discovering the best of the local "bars" as a location for an *aperitivo* and a source to question about a *trattoria* or *pizzeria-ristorante* for dinner. Enna is well supplied. We became particularly attached to a *pasticceria* on the corner of the Piazza Garibaldi, just across from the Prefettura (Court House) and the Questura (the Police Department). It did most of its business at morning and noon, and the five o'clock custom was sufficiently slender to allow much attention to be paid to our needs. Gin and tonic they had, but they were not quite sure about the proportions. My request that they put quite a lot of English gin in my Martini and Rossi dry vermouth was also a source of curious interest, but they were able to meet our extravagant requirement for ice (in March!) and the prices were modest. A request for something to nibble, done mostly in sign language as I couldn't find a proper Italian word for "munchies," resulted in small lacy paper doilies under little glass bowls of potato chips and peanuts. The atmosphere and the temperature were warm and the view out into the chilly *piazza* attractive. The shop was fully decorated for Easter, although it was still only the first week of Passiontide. There were chocolate rabbits and eggs of all sizes wrapped in all colors of cellophane and aluminum foil. All Italian children are given the huge colored eggs for Easter. The pink, pale blue and golden coverings are removed to reveal the chocolate. Inside there are other candies, toys, dolls, small electronic games, space blasters and Barbie.

Guidebooks gave no clear picture of the rank order of restaurants in Enna, so we were grateful for local knowledge that directed us to Da Gino on the Viale Marconi, the nearby edge of the city where the street skirts the cliff that drops away to the north. In Enna's chilly spring we were happy to find that the place was centered about a large brick pizza oven where a man in a white T-shirt, cap and trousers was tending a brisk wood fire inside the beehive *forno a legna*. I think the fire had been going briskly all afternoon, and the pizza chef had some extrasensory way of determining when to shove in a couple of more slender pieces of wood and also of knowing when the temperature reached the exact level for perfect pizza. While our slightly more elaborate *primo piatto* was being prepared, the master of the pizza baked a batch of crust, which he provided with the compliments of the house to accompany our premonitory jug of wine. We watched a steady stream of young businesspeople, well dressed and sometimes with children in hand, who stopped in to order take out pizza to bring home for supper. An increasing number of young Italian families consist of a couple with one child and two jobs. Grandmothers do a great deal of babysitting, child rearing, and often cook the midday dinner for the three-generation family at the three-hour noontime break. Parents take the burden off grandmother in the evening by bringing home the supper in a cardboard box.

The pizza chef performed like a dancer in front of his glowing orange spotlight. His paddle was about six feet long.

He could place the pie nearer or farther from the heat, rotate it to even up the puffy rim and rescue it at the perfect moment, in between punching down the dough for the next order and distributing handfuls of chopped cheese and mysterious sauce on the flat circles laid out on his marble counter. Later we saw him working with an apprentice who, although willing and respectful, obviously had a time yet to serve under the scrutiny of the old *maestro*.

We spent three nights in Enna and had opportunity to visit a number of its most interesting places. I climbed the fortifications of the Castello di Lombardia. Originally built by Federico II, it was remodeled by Frederick III of Aragon, the one who picked up Sicily after the French were ejected at the time of the "Sicilian Vespers" at the end of the thirteenth century. He actually used it as a royal residence when in town, which was probably not very often. There were originally twenty towers, but only a half-dozen remain standing. Climbing stone stairs from courtyard to courtyard, I eventually got to the top and found an open-air theater in some disrepair. It looked like a great place for summer opera, but it cried out for a refurbishing.

Every Italian city has its museum, and most of them have things of wondrous age and beauty on display. Enna actually has two: a small archeological museum, and the little Museo Alessi in back of the *duomo* which houses not only the treasures of the church itself but also the results of a lifetime hobby of an eccentric clergyman, Canon Giuseppe Alessi, who lived from 1774 to 1837. He collected paintings, but most of all, coins. Numismatics had never held much magic for me, but the Alessi collection in Enna changed this. Here displayed in clearly labeled and well-lighted cases are some of the beautiful rarities of the Greek centuries. Classical nymphs and queens are shown in profile on decadrachmas in silver as perfect as though newly minted. The "tails" side of these coins often presents a four-horsed chariot being driven by the goddess Nike, the patroness of ancient victory.

But even rarer is the collection of later coins, the minting of the emperors of Rome. All of them are here, from Augustus in 27 B.C.* to Romulus Augustulus, who met his end in 476 A.D. and was the last of the western or "Roman" emperors. After that the power was Byzantium in the east and the popes began to gather authority in the Eternal City. The little museum devotes a separate case to each emperor, and the very brief biographies that are included tell how they got to wear the purple in the first place and how they met their end. Almost none died in bed, several were quite mad, and except for the remarkable five in a row between 96 and 180 A.D.,† they were, almost without exception, lousy rul-

---

*Remember, Julius Caesar never was an emperor or even undisputed ruler of Rome. Brutus and the gang that cut him down feared that he would end the Republic by becoming King. Augustus, shrewder by half, kept all the forms of republican government but made himself the *princeps,* consul and tribune for life, thus setting up the absolute rule of the emperors for the next 500 years.

†The good ones were Nerva, Trajan, Hadrian, Antoninus Pius, and Marcus Aurelius. They were an unusual lot and included a soldier, a statesman, an architect, and a moral philosopher among their scant number.

ers. Having been only hazily aware of the identities or even the names of many of this extraordinary succession of powerful men, I was pleased to get to know them a little more intimately from the faces on the coins arranged on the orderly buff cushions of the good canon's collection. There are many collections of silver and gold coins elsewhere, but the Alessi Museum has an unusual wealth of the smaller bronze and copper coins that have largely disappeared over the centuries. Coins show us emperors as they wished to be remembered: pious, powerful, severe or handsome. Nero looks quite the fop. Constantine is something of a brute.

Returning down the slope of Via Roma with our heads full of the force and power of the Roman Empire, we met the afternoon *passeggiata* coming up the cobblestones. They were led by the usual arm-in-arm grownups and the pretty young *ragazze* on charming display, while eating great mounds of *gelato* in cones and saying pert things in semi-intelligible Sicilian back to their admirers passing in the other direction. The Piazza Vittorio Emanuele was impassible, being filled shoulder-to-shoulder with young people. We escaped down an arcade next to a bank and discovered the Ristorante Ariston, which had been mentioned favorably in one of the guidebooks. We gave it a try for an early supper but concluded that it was in all respects inferior to Da Gino, where we returned for our finale in Enna the following night; a fine *vitella limone*, a delicate and piquant slice of veal sizzling in the center of a large, hot plate.

But our last full day in Enna was the most memorable. It was Palm Sunday, which initiates a week of ancient ceremonies and processions for Holy Week. Even these preliminaries were impressive. Three successive processions came up Via Roma, passed our hotel, and wound up at the *duomo*, still farther up the way. The first procession featured children, including a half-dozen seven- or eight-year-old girls dressed in the Carmelite habit of the standard statuary of Saint Rosalia. They carried small bunches of roses and seemed very self-assured. There were yard-long rosaries wrapped around their waists. People applauded as they walked by. Immediately behind them came the band, quite gorgeously costumed in red jackets, black trousers and white cross belts. Almost all the musicians were white-haired men, but there were a few teen-aged girls among the flute and clarinet sections.

Each of the three parades was followed by a forty-minute interval while the band returned to the starting point by another route and regrouped to lead the next contingent on the climb up Via Roma. Although not terribly steep, it is a long uphill march and we found it required a couple of pauses for us to get back to the Albergo Sicilia. It didn't seem to bother the boys in the band; they made the full hike three times in the afternoon, blowing mightily all the way. The subsequent processions brought penitents and "children of the Hebrews" in various raiment. Some wore white conical hoods that Americans associate with the Ku Klux Klan but are actually descended from a medieval Spanish tradition that allowed penitents to beat their breasts in public without revealing to friends and neighbors just who was confessing to what. The tradition reminded us of the three or four centuries of ineffectual and inequitable Spanish rule in Sicily.*

---

*It helps to keep such influences in mind by a brief review of who has been in charge of Sicily in the long succession of foreign rulers. Colonizing Carthaginians and Greeks had their millennium before the Romans settled in for their six hundred years. Thence Ostrogoths, Vandals and Byzantine Greeks took turns for a couple of centuries each. The Arabs from North Africa maintained hegemony for a quarter of a millennium before the Norman centuries ensued. The Angevin French were a momentary mishap before the rigid stratification of Spanish society was clamped down upon the island, first by Aragon, later by the Bourbons. Austrians took over in the early nineteenth century and held Sicily for the shortest time. Even Garibaldi, who started at Marsala with his Red Shirts, was not a Sicilian nor was his cause. (He was born in Nice [properly Nizza in Italian] and almost broke with Cavour when that wily politican bargained it to France for Napoleon III's assistance against Austria.) For a long time Sicily didn't choose to be part of a united Italy, and was only persuaded into the modern state with the promise of a "special status," such as that which still dissatisfies the determined Quebecois who, it seems, would prefer a weak economy to remaining a province of a united Canada. The "Unionists" of Northern Ireland also come to mind. In comparison with such destructive irrationality, the Sicilians seem the very epitome of moderation and sensible compromise in spite of the real abuse they have suffered over the centuries.

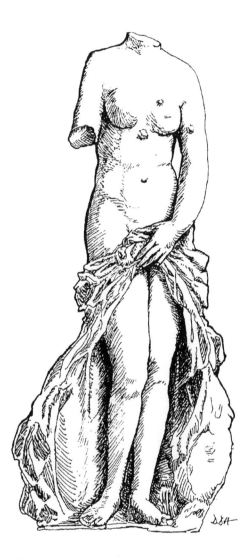

The Venus Anadyome. A first- or second-century copy of a Greek original, the centerpiece of the Paolo Orsi museum. The knobs on the arm, breast and upper body are the points where the arm (held up in modesty) was left attached to the torso by the marble carver.

XI.

TO SIRACUSA

We left Enna early in the morning to meet the scheduled time for returning the sturdy little Fiat to Avis at the airport of Catania before noon. Straight to the east, the four-lane *autostrada* led us directly towards the distant and lofty silhouette of Etna. The great ice-blue bulk was in front, above us or over our shoulder for eighty kilometers, seeming to grow shorter as we got closer to it. I have never really understood the odd optical phenomenon that makes a distant hill seem higher as it recedes from our sight. As the details of Etna's peak became clearer they also seemed to sink closer to the horizon. A few clouds drifted about the summit and suggested the possibility of volcanic activity. There is evidently a considerable amount of heat being vented into the atmosphere most of the time. The trip to the top is no longer a heroic passage. Someday, I hope.

Aeroporto Catania is the second largest in Sicily but not nearly on the scale of the airports of Palermo or the major mainland cities. But it is busy. The Avis lady accepted the keys and went to take a hasty glance at the car, more, it seemed, to figure out where it was parked than to inspect the pretty little thing for wear and tear. I had neglected to refill the tank at the last and this oversight eventually showed up on the credit card charge at the most expensive rate for petrol I have ever experienced. Even so, Auto Europe's arrangements were immaculate and included all the insurance and *chilometraggio*. The Fiat was a miser with the gas, and even though I could never figure out what the kilometers per liter came to, I never felt that filling up the small tank cost very much.

The SAIS bus line runs direct from this airport to various stops in the center of Siracusa, ending up at Riva della Posta in Ortygia, the old and original peninsula of the city. But on the bus we had made the acquaintance of a bilingual guide who was on his way home for the holidays before Easter. With characteristic Sicilian kindness he pointed us to a bus stop in the nearer part of the town that was next to a twenty-four hour cab rank where we could find a ride to our hotel. Siracusa has grown and shrunk many times in its 2,500-year history and now has about 130,000 inhabitants. This is perhaps half or even one-third the size it was back in the heyday of the classical civilization when Archimedes was the famous first citizen of the town. In spite of the population density of the multistory buildings of the modern area, their space does not compete with great areas of the ancient city now left empty as archeological parks, and found in meadows of the surrounding countryside.

On our first visit to Siracusa we reserved at the Hotel

Bellavista, somewhat out of the center of things, but a comfortable spot with large rooms, balconies, spacious lobbies, a restaurant and breakfast room. The public bar and lobby were decorated with high-quality prints of contemporary artists' work, none of it familiar to me. A bus into the center stopped 80 yards down the hill on the Viale Tunisi, where there was also a full complement of city services, laundry, stationers, coffee bars (three of them) and various markets and *alimentari*. We researched the local neighborhood and prepared to take on a full-scale exploration of Siracusa the following day. We had no particular plan as to how long we would stay in this town when we arrived. Perhaps because of this lack of schedule, it turned out to be one of the most pleasant weeks we have ever spent on our travels.

The old part and original center of Siracusa was an island, Ortygia, which basks just offshore in the sunny blue bay now known as the Great Harbor just north of the Gulf of Noto. It is an ideal maritime location with a well-protected anchorage and a nearly perfect climate. Although surrounded by salt water, it is nourished by a unique freshwater spring, La Fonte Arethusa, which bubbles up and supports a small grove of papyrus plants within a few feet of the sea. This supply of drinking water was the salvation of the city in times of siege, and a suitable mythology developed about its source and maintenance. Arethusa was a lovely nymph who attracted the desire of the river god, Alpheus. Diana, the virginal and virtuous, sought to protect her from her romantic fate by turning the girl into a fountain. Alpheus, not to be denied, turned himself into a secret river that flowed into Arethusa invisibly and has provided clear and pure water to Siracusa ever since. The Fontana is on the southern waterfront next to the Foro Vittorio Emanuele II, where the young stroll by day and grownups of the town enjoy their evening *passeggiata*. The combination of easy fortification, a good harbor and a perpetual water supply attracted the settlement of a Corinthian colony from mainland Greece all the way back in 734 B.C., from which date the Syracusans measure their history. The subsequent 2,700 years have not been without problems, and the town may not be what it once was in either size or economic importance, but what a past it was! Siracusa flourished under a republican government and became the largest of the Greek colonies and a center of science, philosophy and commerce. The democratic but unstable government was taken over by Gelon of Gela, who seems to have been a sort of regional strongman with an admirable cultural streak. Gelon became a chosen "tyrant" or absolute leader more by political skill than force of arms. He led the people of the town and their allied neighbors to a great victory over the ever-menacing Carthaginians at Himera in 480.

Hieron succeeded Gelon and presided over the growth of the city, which soon became the greatest center of offshore Greek culture. Pindar the poet and Aeschylus the tragedian came to live here at the court of Hieron. Plato came to stay for extended visits before he set up his Academy in Athens. Another brief interval of democracy intervened before Dionysius the Elder became tyrant in his turn. Athens tried to take the town for some forgotten warlike or commercial reason. It failed with the loss of ten thousand soldiers, most of whom later died as slaves in the underground limestone quarries of Siracusa. The defeat of the Athenian invasion force came despite their having built a double wall around Siracusa on the land side and blockading it from the sea. To prevent the like from ever happening again, the popular tyrant Dionysius the Younger decreed the building of a huge defensive wall miles around to protect the city from further invasion.

Siracusa in this period almost foreshadowed the history of eighteenth century America, the western colony which grew too powerful for its mother country to control.

Later, a nascent Rome made Siracusa an ally. But a fatal mistake was made in the late third century B.C., when the town fathers decided to change sides during the Second Punic War and concluded a pact with the Carthaginians. Rome was closer than they thought, and soon besieged the town. The resident genius Archimedes thought up all sorts of engines of war and fire-producing parabolic mirrors to protect the city. He also produced the first flamethrowers by igniting the natural exudate of the local asphalt mines, and found a way of flinging it onto the Roman ships, where it clung with dreadful effect. But the siege went on for several years until the Romans finally broke in. The Roman commander, Consul Marcellus, gave orders to preserve the life of Archimedes, but word wasn't received in time. The seventy-five-year old genius was run through by a soldier who came upon him doing geometry problems during the sacking of the city.

Siracusa recovered and even flourished as a Roman town, and was a prosperous seaport in the mid-first century A.D. when St. Paul, being brought by sea to Rome for his trial, dropped anchor in the harbor after a fair south wind brought the ship from Malta. St. Luke records the fact that Paul tarried there for three days before going on to Reggio Calabria on his way north. There is a legend that he introduced Christianity to the island, but it seems to me that he would have had to work awfully fast to give it much of a start in the few hours at his disposal before he was hauled off to trial and execution in Rome. Presumably Christianity took root in the late first century or early second century and became popular sometime before Constantine legalized Christianity in the early fourth century. We lack records, but Paul's latter-day followers gave Christianity such a firm hold that Siracusa was one of the thorniest holdouts in the face of the repeated Saracen conquests in southern Sicily seven hundred years after he visited the town. It was perhaps an unfortunate stubbornness, since the Muslims repaid it with a nearly total destruction of the city. A great number of the men were simply put to the sword, and most of the women enslaved. Girls and "the more beautiful boys" were selected for various sorts of service to the new masters of the town. It is a wonder that there were enough survivors to repopulate the area, but a number came back to the ruin to live under the rule of the Islamic population. The Normans were comparatively gentle in their reconquest of the city in the late eleventh century but the greatest days of Siracusa were behind it, and it has since settled into a comfortable third place among the cities on the east coast of Sicily, behind both Messina and Catania. At times in the past it has been three to five times the size it is today. The first-millennium walls of Dionysius enclosed a perimeter at least four times the size of the built-up area of the city today. The ruin of the temple of the Olympian Zeus, once within the city itself, is now in the midst of cultivated farmland to the southwest of modern Siracusa; a disconnected irrigation pipe lies carelessly routed through the grassy relic where only one column stands erect.

Ortygia was connected to the mainland in the medieval centuries. Today an elegant Beaux Arts bridge, the Ponte Umbertino, with balustrades and ornate lampposts, runs between the Porto Grande and the Porto Piccolo, the two sides of the harbor. On the land side the Corso Umberto leads to the Piazzale Marconi and then around the square to the beginning of the Corso Gelone, a gently rising avenue of elegant stores and business buildings leading up toward the more modern areas of the city and the historical wonders of the Neapolis. Outstanding among these is the best designed archeological museum I have ever visited.

There are two surprising examples of modern architecture in the Neapolis, the upper town of modern Siracusa. They spring from quite contradictory points of view that characterize the city today. One is a huge bundle of precast concrete sections that form an inverted trumpet bell that rises to a height of eighty or a hundred feet, and covers a large grass-girt circular space on the south side of the Viale Teocrito. It was designed by the winners of an international competition as a suitable shrine for the *Madonnina*, the small statue of the Virgin that was seen to be weeping by many of the faithful in the early 1950s. Evidently neither money nor critical thinking were any hindrance to the erection of this example of '50s, pre–Vatican II architecture. It is visible from nearly every part of Siracusa, projecting like a remnant of some mid-century world's fair above the tops of buildings and trees from any angle. The miraculous popularity of the site doesn't seem to have lasted quite as well as the concrete; the building was closed and locked on the two occasions when we tried to inspect it. But such faith abounds in Sicily. The daily newspapers were full of accounts of another weeping statue of the Eternal Mother during the weeks we were in Italy. The local bishop was trying to avoid committing himself as to the authenticity of the vision and the Vatican was maintaining a hands-off position, making no comment at all.

Almost directly across the street from the shrine is another modern structure, low of profile and largely hidden among the trees of an archeological park. It is the Museo Archeologico Regionale Paolo Orsi, a cluster of hexagonal pavilions connected into a mosaic pattern of exhibitions of all the prehistory of southeastern Sicily. By contrast it would seem to be a temple of the skepticism of rational science set across the street from the rather extravagant demonstration of uncritical faith.

Orsi surely had great faith too, but his would seem to

have been in the history of man rather than in the finger of God poking into our multidimensional world. He was a powerfully motivated archeologist who began to dig into the surrounding countryside around Siracusa in the early years of this century. Much of his work was concentrated around a half dozen sites that span a period from the earliest agricultural peoples to the flowering of the later Bronze Age, when there were a dozen or more cities in and around the area. He also explored prehistoric sites inland as far away as Enna and the fertile flanks of Etna. The hexagonal galleries of the museum are arranged in order from the prehuman inhabitants (dwarf elephants!) to moated villages at Stentinello, Matrensa, Megara Hyblea and Ognina. Large areas of individual burial caves were found hewn in the soft volcanic rock, many of which are quite visible as you drive through the countryside. The grave goods yield an impressive record of growing civilization and evolving skill in painting and pottery. There are legions of pots of the famous red-on-black ware of ancient Greece, all showing great skill in their decoration.

The glass cases of the museum are equipped with labels in Italian and English, which in itself gave this museum a leg up on most in Italy for us. Lovely Greek vases displayed their entire design by being mounted on slowly turning electrically operated lazy susans. Each room presented the next stage of historical development, because the sites collected were presented in historical order. Within each room, touring the cases clockwise walked us through the centuries of that particular site on our way toward the present day. Presented in this fashion, potsherds of "impressed" pottery, bits of red-and-black glaze, and fragments of terra cotta roof tiles, no less than painted vases and sculpted heads, became a history of a people that had been here over the last five thousand years. We spent two and a half hours at the Orsi museum on our first visit and had to come back to complete the circuit on another morning. The sum of our experience came to a realization that over a period that included most of the first millennium, this small area, earthquake-prone and in some threat from a distant volcano, had been kind enough to its early people to give rise to thirty or forty towns which boasted the beginnings of an urban economy. Elaborate religious rituals were developed, and the burial of the dead has left us a record of much of their commerce and manufacture. They quarreled and warred quite cruelly with each other, but most of all, their civilization was a success that attracted others to their island and led to a great flowering of science, poetry, architecture and sculpture that only died out in the aftermath of the conflict of the two great superpowers that grew up to flank Sicily on north and south: Carthage and Rome. No one even knows the names of all the cities that flourished in this area twenty-five centuries ago, but Kasmeni, Akrai, Eloro, Monte Casale, Canicattini, Kamarina, Scordia, Monte San Basilio, Lico dia Eubea, and Grammichele were among them. Herodotus, Pindar and Thucydides recount that more than 80 cities were destroyed by the Araks in the early first millennium before Christ. By 500 B.C. Siracusa itself was the largest city of Europe, larger than Athens and far bigger than

Rome or Carthage. Somehow its very civilization and cultural success led to its downfall. It became less warlike, more cultivated and eventually decadent, in the very period that Rome was assembling its power on the Italian peninsula and while Carthage was extending its great network of trade all over the western Mediterranean Sea. Caught in their conflict, Siracusa lost its preeminence, its strength and, eventually, its independence. The entire sequence is displayed in the lighted vitrines of the Paoli Orsi museum, beginning with chipped stone blades and hand axes and climaxing in the polished red-on-black ware and decorative sculptures removed from the great Doric temples that are still standing today.

One of the most famous pieces in the museum is the centrally displayed statue of *Venus Anadyomene,* often called the Venus of Siracusa, a Roman period statue derived from a Greek original. Dug up in 1804, she clutches a masterfully carved gathering of drapery to her perfect belly with ineffectual modesty. The arm that originally was poised to cover her bosom has disappeared. She is curvaceous and lovely but, unfortunately, headless.

Rain clouds seemed brooding to the west when we returned to the Hotel Bellavista and I was not surprised to hear a few distant rolls of thunder after we had gone to bed. But I was not prepared for the sound that came next. The sharp single unechoing noise was neither a crash nor a rumble. It was a discrete, almost explosive, 120-decibel bang that did not seem to be accompanied by any vibration or tremor. There was neither preliminary crackle nor ensuing echo.

"Thunder?" asked Cathy, wondering why it didn't sound like a storm.

"I don't know," I replied. "I think it was an earthquake." And then a hard rain started and we went back to sleep. At breakfast the next morning I asked Muhammud, the Tunisian barman and waiter, if he had heard the big noise the night before.

"*Ah, si signore. Un piccolo terremoto.*"

Remembering the number of cities and towns that were totally destroyed by "the big one" in 1693, I wondered how a real, full-scale earthquake might sound. No one in Siracusa seemed the slightest bit impressed by this collision or subduction of the various Mediterranean crustal plates of our uneasy planet. I suppose Siracusa is no more unstable than Pasadena.

Most of the better restaurants in Siracusa are in the old island quarter of Ortygia, and we had only begun to explore it in our first days. As in all parts of Italy, almost any pizzeria can be a *ristorante* as well. We were told, however, of a seafood restaurant that was well-esteemed locally. Called La Finanziera, it was said to be frequented by the business community in the area of the Corso Gelone. We had a mysteriously priced meal that turned out to cost around $50 U.S., when we finally were presented with the penciled *conto* on a scrap of pale blue graph paper prepared by an elderly lady who seemed to be mother of the chef. There was no way of calculating cost in advance, since there was no menu, the bill of fare being recited in Italian by the waiter. Later we learned that all fish-houses are moderately expensive in Italy. Never mind, whole shining fish were presented for our choice and although I can't recall the names of those we picked out, both were beautifully done. The waiter disassembled the bones with skill and grace at a folding stand next to our table. They were *tutto squisito,* as was the spinach done with garlic and olive oil. The wine *della casa* was excellent, and the little cream-filled pastry we shared at the end quite worth remembering even now.

Handbills and posters pasted up on the posts of the *semafori* all around Siracusa announced that the circus was in town and would open the next night in a large open space in the archeological park. Tickets were supposed to be £10,000 but there were newspaper coupons for twofers that seemed to be available everywhere. Determined to experience all there was in this wonderful country, we set out by bus and were rewarded by the sight of a red-and-white striped tent rising above the entrance to a carved cave entry called the "Tomb of Archimedes." There was a huge mob of young people crowding up a broad set of steps that gave access to a set of three ticket windows in a trailer, but there were no formal lines to stand in; one just pushed up the steps as best one could and then tried to edge over in front of one of the *sportelli.* I tried my most polite forms of Italian on the excessively rouged lady in the box office: *Per piacere potrebbe dirmi...* "Would you, if you please, be able to tell me..." I also said I didn't speak Italian well and had no coupons to cash in. She looked at my hair color and produced a pair of tickets for

£6000, presumably because I was a senior citizen and an innocent at the same time. The tickets turned out to be for the third row inside the lowest level of the grandstand. The prancing ponies and llamas were practically in our laps. The single-ring circus had all the authentic sights and smells of buttered popcorn and animal dung that I associated with the similarly tented shows in rural Connecticut in my childhood: lots of horses, a few lions, a half dozen elephants and, of course, the clowns. The high-wire act with six muscular young men and one girl making a towering human pyramid forty feet over our heads was quite satisfactory. Form and content, even the music of the show, were international and intelligible in any language by people of any culture. We loved it.

Immediately in front of us were two young couples, quite fashionably but casually dressed. One of the girls had a baby in her lap. They were obviously enjoying the animal and trapeze acts and responded with gusto to our questions in halting Italian. A little more conversation revealed that the taller young man was a third-year medical student; his wife, a nurse. At the intermission they asked how we intended to get home after the show. I replied that I thought there would be taxis at the circus exit. He said he thought that very unlikely and suggested that they bring us back to the Bellavista which they said was in their general vicinity anyway. The car turned out to be a full-sized Lancia four-door sedan with leather upholstery. The comfortable ride back to the hotel was yet another example of the kindness and generosity of Sicilians towards the strangers in their midst.

But the great adventure of coming to Siracusa was, as we had intended, the experience of the great Greek ruins left behind by the builders, rulers and common people of the fourth and fifth centuries before Christ. A ticket to the entrance of the archeological park admits you to the area of the great quarries, and beyond them to the Greek theater. Originally it held more than 20,000 spectators, or perhaps devotees, since the Greek drama was a form of religious rite in which the audience experienced and relived the primal myths of the people and were, in Aristotle's words, purged of their emotions through pity and fear by the close-up experience of the characters. Aeschylus lived in Siracusa for a considerable time, and several of his plays (quite surely *The Persians*) had their first performances in this very theater. Even with many of the upper semicircles of stone seats destroyed over the centuries, the great dish still accommodates at least 15,000 when summer festival performances are held in alternate years. While we stood near the upper limit of the seating, a guide far below left his group, scrambled down to the open proscenium below and, standing in the true "orchestra" or dancing space where the chorus performed, began to recite in Greek. His high clear voice would have been quite intelligible to all of us high up on the periphery of the theater but, as Shakespeare's Casca in *Julius Caesar* said of Cicero's oration, "It was Greek to me."

In the near vicinity of the Greek theater there is a huge *latomia* or quarry, partially underground, which was the source of both labor and captivity of the Athenian prisoners taken by the victorious Syracusans. According to Thucydides, some 7,000 Athenian soldiers suffered their captivity here and most of them died where they were enslaved, cutting out building stone below the surface of the rock. These quarries are immense and give an idea of how much stone, as well as human suffering, was required to build the ancient city when it housed a population three times the size of modern Siracusa.

There is much to see in the archeological park, including the Altar of Hieron II, a huge stone platform where hundreds of oxen were simultaneously slaughtered, and a good-sized Roman amphitheater where the later, still more bloody-minded masters of the town sought amusement in witnessing gladiators hacking each other to pieces and underarmed hunters combatting wild beasts which were provided as their quarry.

The next midday we found the garden outside of the church of San Giovanni, a roofless ruin that is arguably the earliest-built Christian church in the world. Often remodeled during its history as cathedral and church, it is now roofless and displays mostly barren stone walls from its earlier centuries. There is, however, a lovely stone-mullioned rose window from the fourteenth century that is nearly perfectly preserved. The sunny benches in the park around it were occupied by pairs of Sicilian boys and girls who affectionately shared *abbracci e baci*, happy to be outdoors in the spring sunshine. We followed their example.

The Catacombs of San Giovanni underlie this entire area.

We were taken through a significant portion of them by a dignified English-speaking guide with a large flashlight. I had a pocket torch of my own and it proved useful. The catacombs are vast and of a confusing geometry, with galleries flanking both sides of every passageway, where recesses of eight or ten sarcophagi are accessible at every hand from the central tunnel. There were places for thousands of reposing Syracusans here from the earliest Christian era. When asked what became of all the remains, the guide explained that during World War II all the bones were removed to common graves outside of town so that the catacombs could be used as bomb shelters for the beleaguered population of the city during the night raids of the allied forces preparing for the invasion of the Axis-held city. Our guide was a volunteer and refused to be tipped.

The sign of the presence of the Greeks is everywhere in this town, sometimes covered over with later work, but always recognizable. We repaired to Ortygia on Holy Thursday to attend mass at the *Duomo*, entering it through an elaborate narthex of Baroque columns, statues and cornices. On the facade overhead were flamboyant Baroque figures of Saints Peter and Paul. But entering the left-hand aisle we were confronted with a row of Doric columns half buried in the exterior wall that stretched away in front of us. The tall, fluted supports were topped by unornamented capitals that looked singularly chaste in contrast to the whipped cream and cookie crusts of the exterior of the building. Inspection proved that there was another set of columns on the other side. The central nave was separated from these side aisles by rows of square-sided pilasters supporting round-headed arches that were cut through the central cella of what had been the temple of Athena, built in the fifth century before the Christian era. In between the protruding columns in the north aisle there were a trio of lovely statues of the Madonna and a pair of maiden saints, one of which I was able to identify as being Santa Lucia, a pious girl who rejected a pagan suitor and was, as a result of his frustration, denounced as a Christian. This was in the reign of Diocletian, the arch persecutor of Christians, so she was subsequently killed. Beside her is Saint Catherine of Alexandria, that mysterious Egyptian maid who is always shown with the wheel on which she was unsuccessfully martyred. Legend has it that the wheel shattered and her persecutors had to finish the job by beheading her. The three holy *fanciulle* gave the impression of being little more than teenagers, and thus were easily identifiable as the work of Antonello Gagini or his followers. Standing between the Grecian columns in the quiet of the side aisle, they are marvelously serene.

It seems totally appropriate that this holy space, which has experienced the best and worst of four great religious traditions, should preserve a devotion to such exemplars of female grace. Having been started to honor Pallas Athena, the goddess of wisdom, the daughter who sprang fully armed from the thigh of her father, Zeus, the building was converted to a Christian church after some seven hundred years as a temple of enlightened paganism. Four centuries of Christianity were followed by a quarter millennium of Islamic worship in which no human images were allowed to be venerated. But in the twelfth century, the Roman church came back and the reverence paid to Lucy, Catherine, and Mary herself was celebrated by the charming sculptures we now can see. Somehow it seems appropriate that the house of the wise daughter of the father of the gods should be transformed into a place to honor the *Theotokos,* which is what the Greek Christians called the Jewish girl Miriam, the Mother of God. Among Roman Catholics, one of her attributes is the *Sedes Sapientia,* the Seat of Wisdom. I wonder if the Muslims who worshipped here in the ninth and tenth centuries invoked the memory of Fatima, daughter of The Prophet, one of the four perfect women of Islam and wife of the martyr Ali, the fourth Caliph, whose descendants are the Shia Moslems of today.

We attended the evening Holy Thursday liturgy at the cathedral. By the time the Bishop of Siracusa, Monsignor Giuseppe Costanzo, a relatively young man, had finished his carefully enunciated sermon (which I could almost understand), the evening was well advanced. We left the cathedral a few minutes before the recessional and were able to secure a table in a rather good restaurant just across the square. Like a number of fairly pricey establishments in Italy, this one had a touristic menu at the reasonable rate of £20,000 per person. It was a good dinner, but at this time we had not learned the local method of asking one's waiter to summon a taxi for a return to the hotel. We walked to the nearest known cab rank, where the Corso Matteotti comes down to the ruin of the Temple of Apollo. There were no cabs there. After waving and whistling in vain for perhaps fifteen minutes, we flagged down a car with two snappily uniformed *carabinieri* who, quite characteristically for their position, spoke a good deal of English. It took these genteel guardians of the law about four minutes to locate a cab by radio and dispatch us back to the Hotel Bellavista in a white Mercedes Benz with deep black leather upholstery. We thus learned that all the cabs in Siracusa are radio dispatched, that their drivers hand out cards with the proper telephone number if you ask for it, and that most of the vehicles thus summoned are shiny, new, immaculate, large-scale German cars. After all our years of clunking off the bottom of the unsprung and ancient Dodges and Plymouths of Manhattan, the style, efficiency and comfort of a Sicilian taxi was a wonderful experience.

Siracusa is a town whose fame is behind it, and it seems to have little ambition to go back into competition for world leadership again. Life is enjoyable in this far-southern location and there seems to be a sufficiency of employment and the good things of life to maintain content. It is the sort of place where calla lilies grow unbidden in alleys behind the neighborhood petrol station.

The facade of the Duomo of Noto. From this angle the half-collapsed dome is not visible.

XII.

NOTO & A BOOKSTORE
ENCOUNTER IN SIRACUSA

We devoted one day of our first weeklong stay in Siracusa to visiting the neighboring small city of Noto. In spite of a population of just 25,000, this town is reputed to be replete with the most elaborate examples of Baroque architecture in all of Sicily. Noto came by its distinction in the aftermath of the great earthquake of 1693. Most of the town was destroyed and its ruins abandoned after the disaster. This area, Noto Antica, is a dozen kilometers uphill to the northwest of the rebuilt seventeenth-century city. The new buildings were designed by distinguished architects (retained by the local nobility) Rosario Gagliardi, Vicenzo Sinatra and Paolo Labisi, all of whom were more expert in the creamy confections of the then-popular style than they were in engineering or choice of construction material. The pale tufa has turned buff or even brown with the passing centuries, and the elaborate cornices and balconies have decayed to or beyond the danger point in many cases. Finally, just two years ago, for no apparent reason and without warning, half of the dome of the cathedral simply collapsed in the middle of the night. The late hour was a mercy and there were no lives lost, but the process of repair has scarcely gotten underway several years later. Government funds are involved and the safety barriers around the site are marked with the symbol of local authority: *S.P.Q.N.* * Any public work of this magnitude is sure to attract the greedy attention of the local Mafia family, who will divert appropriated funds into the coffers of the local *Don*. It may take a while to get the *duomo* back in service again.

We inspected the exteriors of several churches (mostly closed) as well as the opera house, Il Teatro Communale, which was also *in restauro*. A single laborer was mixing cement in the street and carrying it into the theater one bucketful at a time to participate in some unknown phase of the work. In need of a map of the town, we sought out the tourist office and discovered that no one there spoke a word of English. Armed with a good map we translated for an attractive young couple who turned out to be Norwegian architects who spoke fair English. We had been told by a tourist we met back in Siracusa that the Trattoria del Carmine was a good bet for lunch. We sought it out at the end of Via Ducezio, close to the Carmelite church which, like many of the churches in Noto, was closed, disused and empty behind its pretty facade.

---

*This blazon, in Noto, is derived from the letters SPQR on the standards carried by the Roman legions in the heyday of empire: *Senatus PopulusQue Romanus,* the Senate and the Roman People.

Service at the trattoria was dignified and leisurely, and the waitress was young, pretty and obliging, providing us with an excellent chilled *acqua minerale gassata* while we waited for the *tagliatelle alla cappricciosa*. Well nourished, we set out to explore the center of the town where there were streets famous for their balconies and palazzi famous for their facades. But Noto seemed a sad, almost tragic city. Rebuilt in luxury after the horrible earthquake, it seems not to have been able to grow up to any success in this era, 300 years later. Its great palaces, its theater and finest churches are vacant and decayed. This stillness of many of the streets made me wish for the happier promise of the buzzing motor scooters that heralded the great economic boom of northern Italy. Not by Baroque balconies alone does man make it in this century.

We traveled to and from Noto on an SAIS pullman bus. I am not sure what Sicilian limited-liability company is signified by these letters. Everyone pronounced SAIS as a single word. Their buses are clean and quite prompt. Cruising along the coast we again passed lemon orchards and the detritus of urban sprawl we had earlier seen outside of Siracusa. There were spring crops of dark green spinach already in the fields along the coastal road through the shore towns of Cassibile and Avola. Modern two-bladed windmills stood still in the windless morning air. I assume they irrigated the cropland when the wind blew. Later in the day when we returned, I noticed a hilltop ruin that looked like a medieval castle. Asking a grey-headed man across from me if he thought it might have been built by "Federico Due," I received a shrug of professed ignorance. A mile later he brightened up and pointed out the shell of a crenelated but obviously nineteenth-century abandoned stone house of moderate size and informed me that it once belonged to *"un marchese!"* (a marquis). I was grateful for the reference but reflected that he seemed to differentiate little between the buildings. History in such an old country has a tendency to be divided into things that came before last year or before the living memory of one's grandparents, and all the rest of time. A risorgimento-era titled aristocrat and a thirteenth-century emperor are both back there someplace, possibly not removed from each other by a great span of time in the era of history since Noah's flood. To him a piece of thirteenth-century military architecture might have been built by Mussolini or by the giants who roamed the earth before the sons of God knew the daughters of men.

Back in Siracusa at the *capolinea* (terminal) of the SAIS on Ortygia, we were tired and in need of some sort of rehydration. Our hotel was a £12,000 taxi ride away and it was only four o'clock in the afternoon. We started up the Corso Gelone and rapidly reached the latitude of the Hotel Jolly, by any measure the most expensive hotel in downtown Siracusa. But the lobby bar looked accommodating and in consideration of our thirst and need of a spot to rest, a couple of Schweppes Tonics with plenty of ice and no gin was a very good bargain for the use of their comfortable deep leather club chairs, sofas and their large and immaculate bathrooms. An hour of such creature comfort restored us and we began to pay attention to our neighbors in the lobby bar, when we heard some clearly pronounced English from a loosely gathered group nearby. A chance salutation started a conversation that revealed them to be a delegation from New Britain, Connecticut, not far from our home. The group consisted of the president of Central Connecticut University and a set of faculty members who were being shown Siracusa in preparation for the establishment of a joint project in oceanography between the two schools. The president's wife had gotten into conversation with Cathy and before we departed I found one of my "Headmaster Emeritus" calling cards to exchange with the U.S. prexy. We then set out to windowshop the Corso and look for a work on Sicilian archaeology at a big bookstore next door.

The bookstore Libreria Diana has a brightly lighted window in front but only occupies a few meters of street frontage. When we got inside, however, we discovered a great depth and several floors of books that covered all levels of taste and areas of human knowledge. My first request for a book on the archaeology of southeastern Sicily elicited an enormous volume that contained color plates of almost everything in the Paolo Orsi Museum as well as the outdoor sites all over the country. It bore a price sticker of £450,000. I explained that I needed something *"piu tascabile"* (easier to put in a pocket), and sent him back to search his shelves for other titles. Our conversation attracted the attention of a tall, rather austere Italian gentleman with grey hair who Cathy thought looked like the actor Ben Kingsley. He commented (in Italian) that he wished his "friend" were here because he knew all the books on the subject and would be of help. We lost track of him but the store clerk returned with a simpler volume that seemed to be written in not-too-difficult Italian and was within my price range. We purchased it, and after looking at a few more things, ventured back onto the Corso Gelone in the gathering darkness. Almost immediately we came upon "Ben Kingsley" coming briskly up the street with another, shorter man with a trimmed black beard and merry eyes. Introductions led to an extensive conversation in English about the books available and the sites of archeological discovery that could be visited in the area. The newcomer pointed out that the Italian book I had purchased was published by Routledge of London and was presumably available in English as well. Oh well, my Italian is not so good as not to let me enjoy having a trot at hand. The sharp-eyed and learned young man with the black beard turned out to be a professor of physics and philosophy at the University of Catania who had taken his doctorate at Berlin and had spent a year at the Institute for Advanced Study at Princeton. The socializing on the street corner went on for twenty minutes and ended with an exchange of calling cards and an invitation to join him and his wife for tea on Easter afternoon. We were delighted to accept his offer to call for us with his car at the Bellavista two days later. I am not sure if the immediate hospitality extended by so many Sicilians came from our improvement in Italian or from my being a tourist from elsewhere who actually wore a necktie.

Sergio Caldarella and his wife Giuseppina (her nickname is pronounced like the English "juicy") received us in a somewhat dilapidated building near the old center of Ortygia. They had purchased what looked like an earthquake-shaken structure at a bargain price and were in process of renewing it. It was already almost completely filled with books and would soon become a *studiolo* and a library for the young professor. The couple's daughter Altaira (named for the star Altair) was a beguiling and energetic two-year-old whose weekend time was not to be denied to her mother, who worked as an accountant during the week. *Nonna* (Grandmother) had charge of Altaira on most weekdays and also gave her daughter strict instructions as to how the child was to be brought up, which edicts Giusi would disobey only at her peril. We ate *Colomba*, an Easter cake in the shape of a dove, and were delighted to discover that the whole family spoke quite good English. Altaira was adept at punching a few keys of the substantial family computer and directing her way through an interactive program on a CD ROM that was teaching her our language as well as her own through the antics of computer-generated, brightly colored alligators and birds who talked back to her in English. Considering her age, I figured she knew nearly as much English as Italian. By the time the afternoon was done we weren't nearly at the end of the conversational possibilities, and I suggested that we have dinner together at a restaurant if Sergio would suggest one.

The restaurant, Orto di Epicuro, turned out to be a good

one* and the *aperitivo* had the effect of improving my fluency in Italian about threefold, so that along with the baby (always an ornament and charter to the best service in an Italian restaurant), we looked a little like slightly dressed-up Sicilians. To the people at the table across the way we blended into the local population, which allowed them to speak English quite unselfconsciously in tones just loud enough for us to understand. Their talk over the *calamari* and *gamberetti* was largely of faculty politics back home, for they turned out to be members of the same Connecticut delegation we had bumped into at the Jolly. On our way out, after dinner, I wished them well in our native tongue and got a shocked look from a biologist.

"Good heavens!" he gasped. "The presumed anonymity of being surrounded by another language may have led me to say something terribly indiscreet about a colleague!"

I assured him that I retained no memory of any slander and was merely glad to see that they too were able to enjoy the admirable seafood of Siracusa, which had added yet one more highlight to an already memorable day. When the attractive young Syracusan couple dropped us off at the hotel they left us with many good wishes for future correspondence and exchange of books, which were happily fulfilled in subsequent months.

---

*A visit to this restaurant a year later was less satisfactory. Not only was the food less good, but the clientele had become sparse. Chef quit? New owner? One of the dangers of mentioning hotels and restaurants in a book like this is the transience of all human affairs. But the location was good and it might possibly have recovered by now.

We spent another day in Siracusa visiting the Regional Gallery in the Palazzo Bellomo in Ortygia, where there is an excellent collection of paintings, sculpture, church vestments, gilded altar vessels and ceramics spanning all of the post-Norman periods of the island's history. The building itself is a thirteenth-century palace, dating from the time of Frederick II and demonstrating that not all of the architecture of the period was military. There are paintings of the Middle Ages here which have found their way to Sicily from Emilia and even from beyond the Alps. There is a fine Caravaggio, *The Burial of St. Lucy*. But the gem of the collection is a badly decayed but still wonderful painting by Sicily's own Antonello da Messina. Painted in the 1470s it shows a great fusion of the Germanic and Italian styles of the *Quattrocento*. Antonello had travelled to northern Europe and learned much there. He also seems to have been influenced by the painters of Tuscany and the Veneto. But here his Angel Gabriel and Virgin Mary are purely Sicilian, luminous, serene and holy, despite the near ruin of much of the surface of the *tavola* on which they were painted.

The abduction of Persephone by Pluto (also known as Dis) may have started out rather roughly, but they obviously got on well; he eventually agreed that she could go home to Mother (Demeter) every spring to inspire the sprouting of the grain. In the opinion of this Greek vase painter, their winter domesticity was idyllic.

XIII.

GRAVES, WARS & RUINS

After our first week in Siracusa we were convinced that there was much more to experience there. We returned for another visit a year later and were not disappointed. This second time we did rent a car and put up at the Hotel Panorama, slightly to the north of the archeological park, uphill from the Corso Gelone. The room was large and the bath equipped with a north-facing window that revealed the distant prospect of Etna, projecting its characteristic plume of smoke in the morning air.

A friend had equipped us with an essay on the true location of the grave of Archimedes that he had downloaded from an appropriate site on the Internet. The researcher described the location as being behind a hotel parking lot a half mile uphill from the traditional site (which is universally described as bogus). He also concluded that it was difficult to visit, since he had been denied entry and had resorted to trying to scale the wall from the car park behind the hotel. I got out the sheets of the printout and discovered that he had been talking about the Panorama, the easy-going hotel where we had booked rooms. Reflecting on the experience of the American scholar, I wondered if he might have approached the hotel in field-trip garb, perhaps blue jeans, khaki shirt and construction boots. Evidently he met with total rejection. Wearing jacket and a floral Italian cravat, I had no trouble when I asked about the Tomba di Archemede and I was led to the Giardino d'Archemede. (When impersonating a professor in Sicily, try to look like one of the local species.) One of the waiters was watering the flowers around a stone-lined recess in the ground where large blocks of masonry outlined a space quite obviously designed to accommodate a burial. All the evidence seems circumstantial, but I am easily convinced that this is the site of the interment that was described by Roman sources after the unfortunate murder of the old scholar during the sack of 211 B.C.

Northwest of the city we spent a pleasant afternoon exploring the broad and largely unpopulated meadowland of Epipolae, where the ancient walls of Dionysius converge from the shores on both sides of Siracusa to join at the location of Castello Eurialo, the old stronghold built to defend the city from inland invasion before 400 B.C. The "Castello" is a mighty fortress with many underground chambers and galleries that allowed a large garrison to threaten any army attempting to pass on their way to invest the city proper. It was evidently important in the successful defense of the town against the Athenian attack. In the following years Dionysius the Younger, the most successful tyrant of Sirracusa, had the great walls constructed, which incorporated the castle, encompassed a distance of 20 kilometers around, and walled off the city from land attack. The walls followed a part of its seacoast as well. This huge complex is still traceable from the crest of the highland. It is the largest and best-preserved ancient Greek fortification anywhere. We were fortunate to meet up with an English geologist and his wife on the site. They shared the fruits of their extensive classical education with us. They were traveling about Sicily camping in the tight quarters of a rather small recreational vehicle while they relived the battles and constructions of the pre-Christian era.

The ruins, fierce assemblies of great dressed stone blocks, reminded us that there have been wars in Sicily since the beginnings of written history and stories about other wars that took place in the mythic memory of man. The lovely island has been invaded countless times, almost always conquered, generally misruled and frequently left in ruins. Our times have been no exception to this pattern, except for the fact that there has been a modicum of local control (not all of it beneficent) left in the wake of the British and American passing through in 1943.

After the 1942 seesaw battles across North Africa had first been checked by the British at El Alamein and finally compressed by the American armies arriving from the west into the bitter and bloody fight for Tunisia, Italy's army had been greatly reduced in effectiveness. A few of Rommel's Afrikacorps of experienced fighting men were gotten across the short strait into Sicily in May 1943, but they left more than 300,000 German and Italian prisoners of war behind them. The Germans lacked the manpower to defend the entire coast of Sicily, and when the Allied attack by both British and Americans came, it was opposed by the Italians but not effectively resisted. First the southern islands of Lampedusa and Pantelleria were heavily bombed and then invested. Allied air dominance made daylight bombing relatively easy, and the need for concealment of the actual site of the landing resulted in great destruction of cities as far west as Marsala. The invasion itself was made, however, in the eastern corner of the island, where Capo Passero projects towards the southeastern Mediterranean and Malta. Montgomery's 1st Airborne Division and Patton's 82nd Airborne dropped on opposite sides of the Cape, and both suffered great losses. Some were air-dropped into the sea, and not a few transport planes were shot down by trigger-happy antiaircraft gunners on their own side. Conventional amphibious landings near Gela and Agrigento on the south coast went better, and the rival generals set out to take the whole island, Montgomery in the east heading toward Messina and Patton moving inland and west to capture Palermo and Trapani. The British got the worst of it, running into the Herman Goering Division, one of the Nazi's best, while Patton had to contend mostly with dispirited Italian troops. The commander of the combined effort, British Major General Alexander, eventually ordered Patton to leave the western objectives until later and to line up with Montgomery along a perimeter that began in Catania, and stretched around Etna to the north coast road that led to Messina. Getting around the east side of Etna is, even from my unmilitary view, a dicey proposition. Montgomery eventually got by it on the west, but whichever side you choose, the Sicilian terrain is a lot easier to defend than to attack. At about this point Hitler decided that his Italian allies were liable to lose the show and sent two more divisions, one parachute and one panzer, across the Strait of Messina to shore up the defense.

It took nearly another month for the Allies to fight their way into a badly bombed Messina. Working mostly at night to avoid the incessant bombing, the Germans withdrew most of their soldiers and almost 10,000 vehicles and tanks before the city actually fell. I can't remember which of the two very capable but prideful generals got into town first, but the nest was empty when they arrived. They spent the rest of the war as rivals.

The whole Sicilian campaign lasted a little more than five weeks, and in effect secured the whole Mediterranean for the remainder of the war. In comparison with some of the bloodier battles of the two great wars of the twentieth century, relatively few lives were lost. I think the smaller battles of Dionysius the Younger may have produced more casualties. Today there is more visual evidence here of the battles of 350 B.C. than those of World War II. Italians have a genius for rebuilding the treasures of past ages when they are knocked down by war or earthquake. A great deal of Catania and most of Messina have been reassembled as more modern cities since

1943. Classical ruins, however, have been carefully preserved by archeologists.

As always is the case when walking the countryside among ruins, we ended up the afternoon in need of something cold and wet. We had passed several sites of what looked like seafront inns on the way to our excursion at the Greek fort at Eurialo. None looked too promising. But on the way south we saw a modest sign pointing to something called "Openlands." Set in among broad meadows behind a large parking lot were a series of low buildings surrounded by lush flowerbeds and ornamental trees. It turned out to be a party house for weddings, confirmations, business conventions or perhaps even receptions for people addressed as *Don*. Although the kitchens were only opened by reservation for catering a large party, the bar was at our disposal and we were served drinks and chips at an umbrella-equipped table on a terrace facing a garden full of Easter lilies and amaryllis. A hummingbird performed near trumpet flowers for our benefit. To the south a sparkling red kite rose up from the fields and flew ever higher over distant Siracusa. At precisely six o'clock the Angelus bell rang in a distant church somewhere beyond our sight.

The mighty rock of Cefalù with Roger II's church at its foot.

XIV.

CEFALÙ & THE EAST

Most travelers circle Sicily in one direction or another. We did it in two stages, once counterclockwise, once clockwise. Cefalù was the first goal of the second voyage. We had come back to Sicily by sea, taking the night boat to Palermo from the Stazione Marittima on the beautiful Bay of Naples. Not being sure of the size and accommodation of these ferries, we took the advice of a travel agent in Naples and reserved a second-class cabin with four berths, thus allowing space for luggage and moving around inside what would otherwise have been petty tight quarters. Besides the two uppers and lowers, the cabin had a lavabo and about as much floor space as would fit the two of us snugly. It was well ventilated and equipped with clean, folded sheets, pillow covers and blankets. All around us were cabins crowded with Italian kids off for a spring study tour of the same antiquities that attracted us, traveling with teachers who wore the same look of mildly harried exasperation that is the usual visage of chaperones of secondary-school students the world over. It took the young a lot longer to settle down to sleep than it did us.

These overnight ferries ply all the major ports of the Mediterranean and provide very inexpensive service for tourists if you calculate that they furnish not only transportation but hotel accommodation for the night as well. For the economy-minded backpackers there are even the *poltrone*, the reclining airplane-variety of seats arranged in serried rows before all-night television replays of current soccer games. We felt that the economy of the second-class cabin was quite enough to justify our dining in the *Ristorante* rather than the *Caffè*. Feeling quite grand, we ascended to the dining salon, where white-jacketed waiters settled us into crimson upholstered chairs amid immaculate napery and elegant stemware for a dinner at least a cut more elegant than we usually afforded ourselves while on land.

The night was cloudy and dark, and no lights were visible on the distant land after we left the harbor of Santa Lucia behind and set out across the Tyrrhenian Sea. Secure in the comfortable bunk that night, I thought of Roger II making the same crossing nine hundred years before in a warship of the eleventh century, a tiny shallop in comparison to the mighty ferry of our trip. On his way back from a successful war with the Pope, Roger was overtaken by a great storm. The seamen were skilled but the seas became mountainous, and a grey dawn brought no diminution of the wind. The storm blew for a day and a night and then again for another day. By the end of a week with the pumps constantly thump-

ing in their wooden shafts and the ship wallowing at the will
of the wind, the terrified sailors were in despair. The king
merely spoke the common sentiment when he recognized
that only God could save them now. He made a solemn vow
in the presence of all on board that if Christ and his Mother
should bring them safe to land—any land—he, the king, would
build a great church to honor the Virgin at that place.

Cefalù, where they eventually came safe to shore, was a
small fishing village set at the foot of an enormous rock, several hundred feet high, which rears up at the edge of the sea.
Here Roger honored his vow and began building the great
church in 1133. Today, approached by road from Palermo, the
cathedral seems dwarfed by the rock behind it, but when you
walk up through the streets of the town from the waterfront,
the rugged Norman towers stand out against the stony backdrop as a monument to faith silhouetted against the great
weight and force of the natural world.

The *piazza* in front of the church slopes slightly uphill
toward the facade, which is itself raised on a terrace a dozen
steps high. We arrived at the end of the considerable uphill
hike to find the church itself closed until three in the afternoon. We spent some time inspecting the outside of the ancient pile and examining the twelfth-century stonework with
care. Hundreds of years of wind-blown dust, sown and fertil-
ized by bird droppings, have created little patches of greenery
sprouting from arches and moldings high on the ancient walls.
Repairs and reconstructions have made a hodgepodge of
stonework in some areas, but the powerful Norman structure

still has its shape and most of its detailing intact. Circular windows in the lower course of the apse are surrounded by round framings that make target shapes fifteen feet in diameter. Golden dressed stone rings are set into the rubble walls, separated by pilasters that are crowned by anonymous portrait heads high above. The exterior of the apse is decorated with interlaced ranks of blind arches, some of which seem to hang from the eaves of the minor apses of the side chapels. Colonnades of delicate capitals and arches encircle the upper edges of the walls. The Norman reputation for creating huge and powerful buildings wherever they went in France, England and Palestine is borne out here again on the north coast of Sicily.

After a *gelato* and an agreeably bubbly *aranciata* at a tilted cafe table in the upward-sloping cathedral *piazza*, we trudged up to the side entrance of the great church and were admitted quite promptly at three o'clock. After the spectacular antiquity, strength and grace of the exterior of the great church, the interior was a mild disappointment. Like many of the oldest churches in Italy, Cefalù was "improved" by considerable redecoration during the popularity of the Baroque style of the seventeenth and eighteenth centuries. In an age devoted to the purification of antiquities, the current administration has peeled off much of this work and attempted to restore the interior to something closer to its original form. There is a lot of steel scaffolding in the transept and an oddly barren look to the nave. But above it all the great half-figure of Christ Pantocrater holds out an embracing arm and a book stating that He is the Light of the world. "He who believes in Me will not walk in darkness." The inscription is in both Greek and Latin, for these are the oldest mosaic inscriptions in Sicily, done in the first half of the twelfth century. At that time the division between Orthodox and Roman communions was not as sharp as it became in subsequent centuries, when the great schism seemed to require fire-breathing mutual excommunications of Roman and Greek Christians. Roger II, although a deeply committed Roman Catholic, was willing to allow the multiplicity of Christian sects and even left his Muslim subjects free use of their mosques in Palermo and elsewhere. The Pantocrater at Cefalù is perhaps the earliest of the medieval mosaics in Sicily and, like the similar one at Monreale, this Pantocrater looks as though he would willingly accept all of his followers without distinction, and surely without an inquisition into their orthodoxy. Beneath him, in the rounded gold background of the apse, stands Mary, hands spread in blessing, flanked by four fantastic archangels whose blue and white wing feathers spread wide on either side of their gilded, dalmatic-cloaked bodies. The messengers of God are far bigger than mortal men, hugely more powerful than anything else in the mosaics save Christ himself and his Mother. Arranged on either side of a rather obtrusive window below Mary's feet are the twelve apostles, neatly labeled, each equipped with some symbol of his life and its meaning.

Cefalù has outgrown its origins as a fishing village and has now become something of a resort town. The beaches along the whole north shore of Sicily are nearly perfect, and this particular stretch of sand looked to us like an ideal place to enjoy the sea and its delicious harvest, as well as the extraordinary example of nine-hundred-year-old architecture. It is also a close visit to Tindari, where there are both Roman and Greek sites to visit as well as the Byzantine Black Madonna.

XV.

TO BRONTE, HORATIO NELSON'S DUCHY

We continued east along this pleasant coast of the island with a large-scale paperback atlas of Italy open in the front seat. This *Atlante Stradale* proved to be a wonderful investment made a few years ago. Not only is it far more complete, and including many more roads than do the Michelin maps; it also opens as a large book and is much easier to handle in the car than the often-folded maps, which are gigantic when unfolded and almost impossible to subdue when it is time to stuff them back in the glove compartment. Seeking a route south to Bronte we branched off the coast road following a sign to San Fratello, and began to climb, leaving the blue of the Tyrrhenian Sea behind us.

The climbing continued for more than an hour through near-switchbacks and hairpin turns. The day grew cooler and the vegetation changed from lemon groves to sparse pasture and eventually to dense forestlands, where we could see wild pigs ambling among the oak groves. A sign alerted us that we were entering the Parco dei Nebrodi, a wild and beautiful range of mountains quite recently decreed to be a protected reserve by a foresighted government. The road traversed pass and saddle, col and cwm until we reached a point where the numbers noted in the atlas told us we were almost 5,000 feet above sea level. The highest of the Nebrodi mountains top 6,000 feet. We could still see the sea behind us, nearly a vertical mile below. The range is separated from Etna by a broad semicircular hanging valley that surrounds *La Montagna* on the west and carries its prodigious rainwater and snowmelt around the inland side of the volcano and out to the sea, both to the north near Taormina and to the south onto the plain of Catania.

As we went up, the oaks were joined by beech and yew as well as hardwoods that were unfamiliar to us. Snowdrifts appeared in the gullies along the road, and marvelous cloud formations drifting towards us from the west suddenly crossed our path to become thick fog banks that our headlights could not penetrate. We passed not more than a half dozen other cars in an hour-long ascent of the mountains. It was hard to believe that we were only a ten-mile horizontal distance from the sea by the time we had risen almost a mile above it. Because of the twists in the staircase road, the trip was close to forty miles long.

Finally we topped the ultimate notch in the foggy woodland and began the descent toward the small town of Cesarò on the other side. Almost immediately the sky cleared and we found ourselves looking up at the cone of Etna. Fifteen miles away across a majestic, well-farmed valley, it was sheathed in snow and studded with outcroppings of black lava rock to a height of 10,670 feet, more than a mile above us. A small plume of white smoke projected jauntily from the crest.

We found Bronte in the gathering darkness and, after some circular navigation of the lower reaches of the town, worked our way up to the lofty location of the Albergo Parco dell'Etna, the only hotel in Bronte. The ebullient and forceful manager seized our bags and installed us in a neat and clean room oddly located one floor below the bar and dining room. When we informed him that I needed a second pillow, that the chamber lacked toilet paper, and that the flush tank would not cease from running, he reappeared with the pillow under his arm, the *carta igienica*, pliers and a wrench in hand, and with a peppy two-year-old following his every move. We reflected that the son was preparing to follow his father's profession. Later, at the bar, the same factotum mixed us a welcome drink of orange vodka, a coffee bean and seltzer water, which he carefully explained was on the house. This at least partially made up for the inexplicable fact that his bar lacked Martini and Rossi dry vermouth and *gin inglese*. There were few other guests, though the hotel was set up to take on tour groups of sixty or more. Most of the staff stood about intently watching the televised close ending of a soccer match between two professional teams that had to be pitting Sicilian honor against all the industrial might of the north. At dinner we met a couple of English-speaking German tourists who were in the process of circling Etna on bicycles; the distance is something more than a hundred miles, with some spectacular scenery along the way. This attractive road follows about the same route as the narrow-gauge railroad, the Ferrovia Circumetnea, that we kept finding across our progress on the following day.

Bronte is a town of less than 20,000, several thousand feet up on the close northwestern shoulder of Etna. It takes its name from the sounds of the thunder that emanate from the great mountain. The onomatopoetic title was also the name of one of the three Cyclops, the one-eyed sons of Gæa, the mother of all the earth. Unlike a number of smaller towns in the area, it has been spared inundation by lava in historic times. But the soils are volcanic here and favor the cultivation of the pistachio nut as well as the grapes that have been made into good wines for a thousand years. This part of eastern Sicily was retaken from the Saracens before the Norman conquest of Sicily by a talented Byzantine general named Georges Maniakes. Georges took advantage of a time of division among the larger Moslem factions to come ashore at Messina in the 1030s. He had a large force with him which included mercenaries from Russia and Scandinavia. One of these was Harold Hardrada, who was at the time working as a sort of hired gun for Zöe, Empress of Byzantium. Harold soon went back north to become King of Norway★ and a pretender to the crown of England as successor to Edward the Confessor. He in-

---

★Hardrada was the descendant of the graphically named king Harold Bluetooth of Norway. One of his great-uncles was surnamed Bloodyaxe.

vaded Northumbria in 1066 but lost out to the forces of Harold of England at Stamford Bridge, where he was killed. In the process, however, he so stretched and exhausted the English that they were unable to pull together and repel William the Bastard of Normandy, who landed in the south and met them at Hastings a scant two weeks later. So for the first of many times, the fortunes of the two great islands north and south of Europe were linked in the adventures of the Northmen who came to rule both realms.

Maniakes took charge of the greater part of eastern Sicily and evidently was responsible for rebuilding some of the defenses of Siracusa that the Moslems had destroyed a couple of centuries earlier. He was a capable general and had already extended the faltering Byzantine hegemony to much of Asia Minor and Syria, fighting the Seljuk Turks as far east as the banks of the Euphrates in the preliminary battles of what was soon to become the First Crusade. But the proverbial politics of Byzantium precipitated his recall from Sicily to Constantinople, leaving the island to the resident Arabs and its approaches to Moslem pirates from North Africa, who were contesting with Genoa and Pisa for control of the Strait of Messina. For the ten or twelve years that he occupied the area around Bronte, he is remembered in the name of the village of Maniace, where "Giorgio" built an abbey for Basilian Greek monks, which was later mostly destroyed by one of those seemingly inevitable Sicilian earthquakes. The Arabs allowed Greek monasteries to continue to exist in Sicily, and the religious foundation evidently carried on for a time. But

Maniakes was the last of the Byzantine Greeks to hold sway on the island. Within twenty years of Maniakes' departure, Robert the Guiscard de Hauteville and his brothers had begun the Norman invasions that would eventually displace the sway of Constantinople and subject the Moslems who did not emigrate back to Africa to the efficient rule of the two Rogers. Margaret of Navarre, Roger II's queen and the mother of William the Good, a deeply pious Roman Catholic Christian, rebuilt Maniakes' monastery as a convent in 1173. The abbey church of her foundation survives with some alteration to this day. It is a pretty building inside the compound of Castello Nelson.

Thus there was plenty of military and religious activity in this inland region eight or nine centuries ago. But Bronte gained its more recent fame from being gifted in gratitude by King Ferdinand IV (sometimes numbered I) of The Kingdom of Sicily to the British Vice Admiral Horatio Nelson, who stopped by in 1799 to help the king back onto his throne whence he had been displaced by Napoleon's Parthenopean Republic. Ferdinand was one of the last of the Spanish Bourbons who, like their French cousins, forgot nothing and learned nothing as a result of their experiences. He and his Austrian wife, Maria Carolina, had to be rescued again later on in 1806 and moved to Palermo, which was firmly under the control of Nelson's battle fleet. It was during his earlier sojurn in Sicily that Nelson, wounded but gloriously victorious at the Battle of the Nile, lived with the British ambassador, Sir William Hamilton, and began his famous affair with

Emma Hamilton, the ambassador's lady. King Ferdinand was grateful to be rescued, and perhaps also was influenced by his royal wife's close friendship with the beautiful young Englishwoman who became Nelson's mistress;* though the English king made Nelson a baron for his efforts and triumph in Egypt, the King of Sicily made him Duke of Bronte, a title which far outranked his English honor and brought a lot of Sicilian real estate with it. He signed himself "Bronte" for the rest of his life, although he later altered it (when the English made him Lord Viscount) to "Nelson and Bronte."

Horatio Nelson had no legitimate descendants; his daughter Horatia, by Emma Hamilton, was largely ignored by the grateful English government after his death at Trafalgar. His brother inherited the dukedom in Sicily; his daughter, Nelson's niece, brought it with her as dowry when she married the Viscount Bridport. The Bridports enjoyed the bounty of their collateral ancestor's heroism for a number of generations until 1981, when a later viscount sold the place to the Commune of Bronte. Sporadic restoration is going on to make it more tourist friendly, and perhaps useful as a retreat or conference center.

We drove up the little tree-lined valley following the signs to "Castello dei Nelson" and parked in a courtyard next to the Good Queen Margaret's convent chapel. There being

---

*This extraordinary *mènage a trois* took place in a striking Chinese folly located in the Parco della Favorita in the northern part of Palermo. It is said that the king built the startling piece of *chinoiserie* to redeem a wager made at an expensive game of bezique.

no one about, we explored the rather elegant if somewhat overgrown gardens before trying to gain access to the house. A modest memorial cross of a knobby Celtic design in the courtyard bears an inscription "Eroe Immortal Nilus." Other than that there is very little to suggest a memory of the British admiral who never lived to take possession of his sizeable property, or even see it before his death. There is a contemporary swimming pool below the garden and other evidence of the good life enjoyed by the owners. We were allowed into the partially restored house by the caretaker, who seemed impressed with my limited ability to discourse on Nelson's career and amours in Italian. Bedrooms are being redone in flowery English wallpaper. The bathrooms are absurdly large and fitted out with huge tubs and washbasins. The walls are currently barren of the paintings that were hung there a few years ago. Perhaps it will be a more interesting spot to visit after a few more years of leisurely restoration.

Across from the house, the chapel of Queen Margaret's convent is an austere but pleasant spot. Its thirteenth-century doorway has a solidity and grace that connects the site with a time far before the major battles and petty quarrels of the Napoleonic era. Various statues and paintings inside range from a Greek icon to the sentimental Baroque figures and the bloody agonies of realistic eighteenth-century representations of the bruised and bleeding bodies of Christ and His martyrs. The early Byzantine icon of the Virgin and Child was brought from the east by Giorgio Maniace himself in the eleventh century. Other signs would seem to evidence at least occasional Anglican practice in this often-exchanged chapel.

One of the more recent memorials is in both English and Italian. It commemorates one Samuel Grisley:

> FRIEND, AGENT, AND FAITHFUL SERVANT OF THE
> DUCHY OF BRONTE
> AND WAS ERECTED WITHOUT UNDUE MODESTY
> AS A TOKEN OF SINCERE ESTEEM BY
> VISCOUNT BRIDPORT, DUKE OF BRONTE.

Grisley evidently worked at the great estate for fifty-two of his sixty-six years, until his death in 1874. Somehow, crediting the memorial's existence to the chap's boss seemed a somewhat lofty and removed gesture of the British aristocracy of the nineteenth century, trying to do something nice and appropriate, but making the otherwise gracious act seem patronizing and self-serving.

The monastery garner has been restored with massive roof beams, and about half of its floor area has been excavated to reveal the foundations of Roman-era buildings that stood on this spot well over a thousand years before the Norman queen located her nuns beside the volcano. Wherever we went in Sicily we kept running into this layering of civilizations that stretch back close to three thousand years. So many have wanted a piece of this precious Mediterranean real estate; many have stayed on to rule its indigenous people without their participation or consent. Most of Sicilian history is a series of accounts of the adventures, successes and failures of the non-Sicilians who have come here to profit and rule.

The great snow-topped bulk of Etna towers above the ruin of the Greek theater of Taormina.

XVI.

TO LINGUAGLOSSA, MESSINA &
TAORMINA ABOVE THE SEA

Heading on to the east, we skirted the north flank of Etna, which kept disappearing into lofty cloud banks and then emerging, seeming higher each time. More confusing optical illusions. Here, looking at the north face of the massif, there was more snow and less rock showing. A flock of white goats approached us when we stopped to photograph the mountain. Failing the peak which kept disappearing in the clouds, I took a picture of the snow-white goats as they scattered up the rocky banks of a stream bed beside the road.

We crossed and recrossed the narrow-gauge railroad tracks of the Ferrovia Circumetnea, which is a sort of scruffy if streamlined Toonerville Trolley, blemished with contemporary graffiti, ambling peacefully through the valleys that encircle the mountain. It runs through vineyards and pistachio orchards, pokes through a few short tunnels in the ancient lava flows, and stops at a village every four or five miles. The line does not seem to haul freight and may have been built as a tourist attraction from the start. It uses the greater part of a day to make a full circuit, but with a well-filled picnic basket and a bottle of wine it should be a pleasant excursion.

By midday we reached Linguaglossa, a pleasant and simple town of 5,000 which boasts a two-star hotel and has an attractive market square where a lone, elderly vendor of oranges watched over his fruit while he sang Sicilian love songs to whoever happened by. Since we were the only ones who passed his cart, he continued to sing to himself in a strong voice after we left to seek a *pasticceria* for something to eat. The proprietor was a dignified gentleman who had a great variety of pastries for sale, but also produced some premade pizza and onion rolls which he zapped in a microwave oven for our lunch. With an Italian beer, Nastro Azzurro, it made a reasonable repast. We questioned how he kept so many varieties of pastry fresh, and learned that the Sicilian pastries are so sugared that they will last for months if kept reasonably cool. He also provided us with a sample of his pistachio pastry. It was wonderful. We had him fill up a box to bring to our acquaintances in Siracusa and felt well-served by this small town. The gentle *pasticciere* had a large portrait of St. John Bosco affixed to the wall behind the cash register. Bosco too was a gentle fellow; he spent his life in assisting abandoned boys and setting them on the road to a productive life. He is one of those numerous saints canonized in the nineteenth century who seem to have led reassuringly virtuous lives but not to have left a profound theological mark on my consciousness. I don't know the source of the pastryman's devotion to the good priest, but he had somewhere acquired dignity and kindness along with a knack at the bake oven.

Our next destination exemplified no such simplicity of spirit. Taormina has been a playground of the rich or the ideal site for an assignation for many centuries. It is a spectacular location, girt round with views of mountain and ocean, and equipped with half the luxury hotels in all of Sicily. We approached it from the south, having just descended from the valley that encircles Etna. Following the signs, we plunged through a tunnel and then immediately exited the *autostrada* to climb the cliffs again to reach Taormina. The highway which had run inland of the beach towns actually goes through the tunnel beneath the famous resort. Starting up from sea level, the vertical climb to Taormina proper is probably three or four hundred feet, enough to require a serpentine roadway on stilts which weaves in and out of the cliffs, as well as a funicular for bathers or beach walkers who wish to transit between the hotel zone above and the shore. We had reserved at the three-star Villa Fiorita, specifically because it was advertised as having a lift, the lack of an elevator in a town as precipitous as Taormina being problematic.

The somewhat gloomy-visaged *impiegato* at the desk received our passports and seized the bags to lead us up to our room. I was not too startled by the short staircase which brought us to a comfortable lobby one flight above. We were a little more surprised to find a cascade of breakfast rooms, card rooms, music rooms and sitting rooms spreading out from the crest of each of the seemingly endless flights of broad, carpeted steps as we worked our way upwards through the building in search of the promised *ascensore*. Cathy later counted a total of sixty-five steps to a modest vestibule where there actually was an elevator to raise us another two stories to our room. There the vertical challenge was almost forgotten in the face of the balcony-embellished room that gave upon the eastern Mediterranean. The rounded toe of the Italian boot was clearly delineated on the horizon, twenty miles away across the mouth of the Strait of Messina. Castel Molo towered over our inland shoulder. The beach towns of Taormina-Mazzarò and Giardini-Naxos stretched along the shore far below. The next day we walked towards several of the more elaborate hotels and tested the bar at one of the larger ones, the Miramar, which sported a blazon of four stars. Far below I could see a diminutive sloop reaching north towards Reggio and Messina. The drinks and view were first-rate, but we had no temptation to sample the expense of their accommodation.

Taormina is close to being a one-street town with various side branches and stairways leading up and down from the Corso Umberto I. The Corso is closed to traffic virtually all day long and is usually teeming with visitors. Since the town is entirely dedicated to tourism, there are lots of restaurants, antique shops, banks, travel agents and coffeehouses. There is even a reliable two-day laundry and dry cleaner at the western end of the Corso in the Piazza Duomo. I was up early on the Saturday morning before Palm Sunday to revel in the copious hot water and well-tiled ambience of the

American-sized shower that the Villa Fiorita provided. Every
so often it is a pleasure to revert from the quaintness of the
Italian *doccia* to the comparatively sybaritic sort of ablutions
that we are so used to in America. Thus inspired to enjoy
Taormina, I walked the length of the Corso without passing
another soul until I reached the *piazza*. Here finally I found
an open coffee bar as well as a gathering of men and boys
outside, who were busily braiding bulbous shapes of crosses
and vases from pale green palm fronds. Tomorrow would begin the remembrance of the passion of the Lord. I was unable
to find a newspaper early in the day in this town devoted to
entertaining people who are on vacation, so I settled in an
overstuffed armchair in one of the tiered lobbies of the Villa
Fiorita to write up our neglected journal. Across from the
window, overstuffed and clumsy pigeons traded places on the
parapet while the males made ineffectual attempts to mount
their chosen consorts. Nothing seemed to be coming of it.
Meanwhile the exhibition was watched hungrily by a pair of
well-nourished feral cats.

   At the nearer end of the Corso, the Via Teatro Greco
projects out along a spur of the mountain to one of the best
sited classical constructions in all of the Mediterranean. The
theater has been much degraded by the ruin of time since
the great tragedies were given here. It has been partially restored over the years that Taormina has been a tourist town,
and is still a wonderful place. We climbed the semicircular
rings of stone seats and looked down to where the dancing
chorus had performed. Behind the openings in the *skene* the

deep blue southern Mediterranean gleamed in the afternoon light. Above our right hand, Etna, cloudless for once, was a blue-and-white pyramid trailing a white trace of volcanic smoke off towards Libya. The mountain dominates the scene of all of eastern Sicily the way Fujiyama does in central Japan. Afterwards we walked the Corso and heard the by-now familiar tenor voice of Andrea Bocelli singing "It's time to say goodbye...." By the time we came home he was popular in America too. We found a simple bar with a broad window where we could observe the town and its people while we had our *aperitivo*. The place seemed to be largely frequented by Italians (rather than French and German visitors or Americans like ourselves). It was comfortable and clean, so we chose from the simple menu and found an excellent dinner. We failed to note the name of this pleasant, inexpensive place, but it is located just where the Via Luigi Pirandello reaches the north gate of the town, La Porta Messina. More specifically it is across the square from the church of Santa Caterina, which displays statuary that would seem to be by one of the Gaginis. All in all, an agreeable venue.

Before turning in for the night I ventured out onto the balcony again. The Italian coast was delineated by lights running from the tip of the toe up to Reggio Calabria. The Sicilian side was even more clearly marked. It appeared to be a chain of streetlights that could guide mariners through the Strait of Messina, perhaps clear of the dangers of Scylla, the rocks on the Italian side, and Charybdis, the voracious daughter of Poseidon who, having been thrown from Olympus into these waters as a thunderbolt by Zeus, became a whirlpool that sucked in the waters and spewed them out again to the destruction of many sailors of the Homeric era.

In the companionable breakfast room of the Villa Fiorita we found ourselves surrounded by Americans, a rarity in a Sicilian hotel. A group of five dignified ladies from Hartford, Connecticut, were enjoying a sumptuous breakfast when we came in; we were later joined by an attractive young couple, both newly minted doctors on vacation from Pittsburgh. They knew scarcely a word of Italian but were getting around very well. We concluded that they were traveling too rapidly and too far in the short time they had free. They had missed both Monreale and Agrigento during their few days on an island studded with the greatest of Greek temples and Norman cathedrals. We later took to lecturing other tourists on what they <u>must</u> visit while in Sicily. Months after we came home I received a postcard of far-Eastern flowers from a young Japanese woman to whom we had given precise instructions as to what she should see in Palermo. She was grateful for what she saw but slightly sad because she felt she could not go to the opera for lack of a proper dress. I guess everybody has some sort of hangup or other. As much as I recommend being a dressed-up tourist, for heaven's sake *(Santo Cielo!),* don't let your clothes limit your chance to see anything on this wonderful island.

Determined not to give the northeastern quarter of the island the same short shrift, we explored Taormina with some care. It has a tidy little cathedral with some good sixteenth-

century sculpture in it. We also visited the beach town of
Mazzaro at the foot of the cliffs. But we chose to use the
town mostly as a base for a slightly more distant exploration
of the museum at Messina, forty miles up the coast. The trip
was quick on the *autostrada,* and terminated in an only mildly
confusing process of finding the Museo Regionale on the
shoreside streets of the town. Much of Messina was destroyed
while Patton and Montgomery were pressing the Germans
from both sides in the summer of 1943. Not all the rebuilding has been graceful. But the location of the small city on
the strait separating Sicily from Calabria, the south tip of Italy,
is delightful. I am always charmed by seaports, even the modern commercial ones. This strait, now spanned by lofty power
cables, might someday be the site of the greatest suspension
bridge of them all. It has been planned but not financed.
Busy ferries ply the three-mile waterway, some of them carrying railroad trains that come from Naples, Rome and the
north of Italy.

The regional museum is small and only able to display a
fraction of the collection for now. An enlargement is planned
and needed, but what is currently displayed is choice. The
hometown exemplar of the arts, Antonello da Messina, is represented by a splendid polyptych of the Madonna enthroned,
wearing a richly brocaded mantle. The work was done for
the Convent of St. Gregory in 1473, thus demonstrating that
the great Tuscan inventiveness in painting in the Renaissance
was well established in Sicily before much had happened in
Rome. Someplace along the line I learned that Antonello

had spent some years in Germany and added that tradition of severe portraiture and fine detail to the liquid Italian ladies of the *Quattrocento*. Later periods are also well represented in this collection, particularly Francesco Laurana's sculpture of the *Madonna col Bambino* and Girolamo Alibrandi's badly damaged but still marvelous 1519 version of the presentation of the child Jesus in the temple.

Until we visited this museum I was unaware that there were two painters known as "Caravaggio," the first named Polidoro, of the early sixteenth century, whose stunning painting of the adoration of the shepherds is one of the gems of this collection. The other and more famous Caravaggio, Michelangelo Merisi, is the great innovator of post-Baroque painting, the Caravaggio who misbehaved himself all over Italy in the early seventeenth century. He was actually on the lam for a murder rap when he did some of his greatest work. Here he is represented by two dark and mysterious paintings: another *Adorazione dei Pastori* and a *Resurrection of Lazarus* that shows Christ stretching forth a red-clad right arm to command life back into the body of his friend who, far from being in the tomb where "he stinketh..." is being presented to the arms of his weeping sisters, Martha and Mary, in a darkened space of what must be a sort of catacomb. Despite the variation from the fundamentalist version of the tale, the intensity of expression of the men lifting the still-lifeless body of Lazarus tells the story of the miracle quite clearly. There is a huge change in human sensibility between this painting and the great thirteenth century mosaic of the same scene at Monreale.

Caravaggio painted in both Naples and Sicily before he died, quite young, in 1610. His works changed the whole thrust of painting after his time, and he influenced a host of followers. Perhaps most caravaggiesque of these was Alonzo Rodriguez, who worked in Messina and whose *Meeting of St.Peter and St.Paul* shows the two towering figures of early Christianity in the hands of their executioners on the way to their final encounter with the love of their Master. Both are stripped naked but wrapped in cloaks that are tied around their waists with rope and chains. Their legs and feet are bare. They lean towards each other, almost close enough to kiss. They look surprised to see each other. Their bodies are bent and constrained by the executioners, one of whom stares with wonder at the relationship between the elderly, condemned men.

At the end of the circuit of the museum, which concluded with an enormous and elaborately gilded four-door coach belonging to the Senate of Messina of the mid–eighteenth century, we found our way north along the port and inspected the Calabrian coast across the way before we turned inland and crossed to the northern side. We drove a dozen miles or more to the west, in the direction of the Milazzo peninsula, peering out to sea to catch a glimpse of Lipari, Panarea, Vulcano and the other Aeolean islands, beloved of Homer, the current jet set, and several film directors. Stromboli, farthest offshore, is invisible from the coast, but in clear weather can be seen from the crests of the Nebrodi Mountains whence the other active volcano, Etna, can sometimes be seen at the same time in the opposite direction.

We took the old road through the shore towns rather than driving the *autostrada* that runs among the mountains slightly inland. Eventually we abandoned the idea of going all the way to the Milazzo peninsula and turned toward the sea in the direction indicated by a sign proclaiming "Ristorante." As seems to be inevitable in Sicily, we were rewarded with good food and a pleasant location for lunch. Like all Italian cooking, Sicilian cuisine depends on the quality of its produce rather than on the sophistication of its sauce. Good oil, good bread, locally grown tomatoes (although Tunisia is "local" to Sicily), fish from a neighboring ocean and a few sprigs of *basilico*, together with wine and cheese, can be found combined in a hundred ways to delight the heart and the palate. We drove back to Taormina rapidly by the high road, hoping to get there before we were overpowered by the need for a nap.

Fish has always been a delight to Sicilians. This famous vase from Cefalù, made in the fourth century B.C., depicts a fishmonger cutting up a tuna with a broadsword.

XVII.

CATANIA & HOME

Finally, after a last exploration around Siracusa, it was time to board a plane and head north again. Our trips to Sicily have always ended at the Catania airport. We have taken buses from nearby cities or brought back a rental car to this location. It is a small but busy terminal that works very well. Once we had to approach it on Easter Monday, when most of Italy was shut down for a day of recovery. The bus schedule from Siracusa required a very early departure, and we arrived in Catania several hours before our plane to the north was scheduled to leave. We had not intended much of a visit to Catania in any case, but on that and a subsequent occasion we found an obliging taxi driver who was willing to give us an hour-long tour of the city for £70,000, around $40 at the time. He was an excellent guide and got us to the Roman amphitheater; the house of the great opera composer, Vincenzo Bellini; the opera house itself; the *duomo*; the Roman elephant

with an Egyptian obelisk on his back; the lava shores of the
north end of the town; and the classy hotels along the sea.
Catania is reputed to be more under the control of Cosa
Nostra than any other city on the island. It also has first class
opera. Beyond these distinctions it has the most aggressive
drivers in Sicily. We had near misses with a number of them
during our speedy trip around the town. Mount Etna stands,
more menacing here than from the west, at the head of a
great avenue, the *Via Etnea*, which runs north through the
city. Our driver explained that Catania has been destroyed
nine times in memory: four times by war, twice by earthquakes, and three times by eruptions of the great volcano. I
am sure Catania would be worth a real visit during its opera
season. According to the guidebooks there is also a spectacular celebration for the feast of Saint Agnes (Sant'Agata) from
February 3 to February 5. The Museo Civico has considerable work of the period of the Spanish Bourbon monarchy,
as well as the Hellenistic and Roman sculpture that comes
up out of the ground in Sicily *come prezzemolo*, like the ubiquitous parsley.

On another occasion a taxi driver took us to see the
duomo and to enjoy an early lunch at a nearby *pasticceria*. He
too got us back to the *aeroporto* with time to spare before our
flight. With our minds full of the mixed melancholy of the
sadness and beauty of the island, we rose into a gentle east
wind and crossed to Reggio Calabria on the toe of mainland
Italy. But as we banked and turned to the north we recrossed
the Strait of Messina and were able to look back to the south-

west, where the great shape of Etna rose almost as high as our newly achieved altitude. The great geographical symbol of Sicily wasn't putting out much smoke from its fumarole. We had asked one of the natives about the violence of the current activity; he had commented that *"Si sveglia solamente un po',"* she has only awakened a little bit. By this time, like adopted Sicilians, we were beginning to feel more affectionately acquainted than awed by the great pyramid of rock, fire and snow. Then the pilot set a course more directly to the north and we turned our backs on the great triangle of this wonderful ancient island.

FINIS

The Norman Rulers of Sicily
And their Hohenstaufen Successors

Tancred de Hauteville

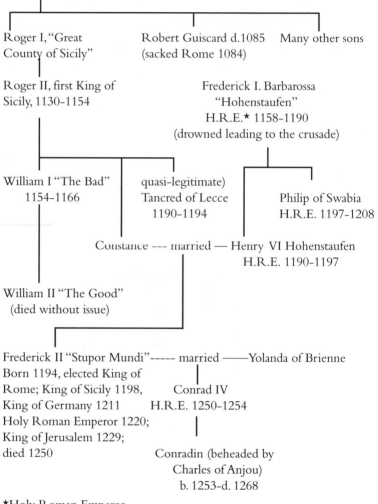

Roger I, "Great
County of Sicily"

Robert Guiscard d.1085
(sacked Rome 1084)

Many other sons

Roger II, first King of
Sicily, 1130-1154

Frederick I. Barbarossa
"Hohenstaufen"
H.R.E.★ 1158-1190
(drowned leading to the crusade)

William I "The Bad"
1154-1166

quasi-legitimate)
Tancred of Lecce
1190-1194

Philip of Swabia
H.R.E. 1197-1208

Constance --- married — Henry VI Hohenstaufen
H.R.E. 1190-1197

William II "The Good"
(died without issue)

Frederick II "Stupor Mundi"----- married ——Yolanda of Brienne
Born 1194, elected King of
Rome; King of Sicily 1198,   Conrad IV
King of Germany 1211   H.R.E. 1250-1254
Holy Roman Emperor 1220;
King of Jerusalem 1229;
died 1250   Conradin (beheaded by
                Charles of Anjou)
                b. 1253-d. 1268

★Holy Roman Emperor

APPENDIX

Customs and Considerations for Travel in Sicily

When you first come to Sicily, you will find that some things are a little different from the north of Italy. To begin with, it is less crowded and things move at a slower pace than along the Via Emilia and in the Po Valley. Life is less *frenetica* than in Florence or Milan. In the countryside we felt a bit more like curiosities or objects of interest to Sicilians than we had been to the Romans. Sometimes the Sicilians stared at us on buses as though we were a zoological exhibit towards which they displayed a passive interest. There is less traffic and the drivers are more accommodating here (except in Catania). All of the petrol stations shut down for a good two hours or more in the middle of the day. Gasoline seems a little less astronomical in price here, near the oil fields and refineries, than we found it to be north of Rome, but do rent a small car. Automatic transmissions are available but not common and demand a higher per diem price. Tickets for city buses are available at the local *tabacchi,* which is marked with a large black-and-white "T" near any bus stop. Taxis are a good value, almost always clean modern vehicles, and drivers are reliable and good sources of information about the town, shops and restaurants. But cabs don't cruise; you (or your hotel or restaurant) must summon them by phone. Driving a taxi in all of Italy is much more of a life career than it is in the U.S., and the drivers would be pleased to see their sons succeed them in the family profession. Intercity buses are large, designated as *pullman,* usually prompt, inexpensive and clean. Trains, as they are in all of Italy, are generally a good bargain. Take *seconda classe* for local travel at least, it is indistinguishable from first class. For the long trip from Naples to Messina or farther into Sicily, however, a reserved seat or even a *cuccetta* (a bunk) will be a lot more comfortable than the rather vertical seats on the trains with more frequent stops. The long-distance trains designated as EC and IC (European Community and Inter City) have better compartments and make the fewest stops, but cost a good bit more than the usual second-class rates we favor on Italian trains. The Ferrovie dello Stato, or FS, is so cheap that the various rail passes are unrewarding in a region as small as Sicily. The Eurail Pass provides a discount from first-class fare; in most cases, second-class fare is as good a bargain.

Among the many ways of traveling to the island, we found the overnight boat from Naples to Palermo the most pleasant and the quick flight from Rome to Punta Raisi (Palermo's airport) the most efficient. Trains take a long time, and the length of the 500-mile drive south through Calabria seemed daunting to me.

Hotels are less expensive in Sicily than they are north of Naples, and sometimes they have less elaborate accommodations. We often traded up a star in making our selections and ended up paying about the same amount for roughly similar quarters. Even so, some of the two-star hotels in the north end of Palermo are a very good value even if they lack the color TV that comes with the *terza stella*. Remember that in any case a two-star hotel will be clean, safe, and able to provide you with a private bath or shower (*doccia*) and ample towels. Lots of towels are a necessity to dry the floor, since most Italian showers lack a sill to confine the water to the drain. Many hotels are equipped with bath towels made of the *nido d'ape* (bee's nest) weave of cotton, like piqué, but not very absorbent. You will need several. Hotels that do not include breakfast (*colazione*) in the charge are always located close to one or more coffee bars that can provide you with breakfast, lunch, or cocktail.

In the tourist off-season, *bassa stagione,* reservations at restaurants are not as obligatory as they are in northern cities, although they are happily acknowledged by the *proprietario* if the restaurant is small or your party large. The huge buffets of antipasto are often the substance of a meal in itself, if combined with a *pasta* or *ministra* from the collection of *primi piatti* on the menu. Many *trattorie* and simple *ristorante* have no menu at all; waiters will recite the bill of fare, usually without quoting prices. Don't be shy about asking *"Quanto costa?"* about anything he suggests, although you will probably find that all of the items among the *primi* or *secondi* are generally priced within a few thousand lire of each other, so the differences are usually less than a couple of dollars. From our experience, no one will try to take advantage of your ignorance or confusion. Most pocket dictionaries or phrase books include a "menu decoder."

Cash is easiest to come by in Italy by using a Visa or Amex card in Bancomat automated teller machines, which are located outside of most large banks such as Banca Nazionale del Lavoro and Banco di Sicilia. If you settle the account promptly when you get home, the machines give a better rate of exchange than traveller's checks, even if they charge you for the cash advance. Debit cards provide the best exchange rates. Almost all hotels and city restaurants will also accept Visa and Amex; MasterCard not so often. A number of the Bancomat machines seem to list Cirrus or Honor access, which will also allow you to draw money from your account at home.

All Italian shops give a receipt *(ricevuta)* for every purchase, even for a cup of cappuccino. The purpose of this is to assure that the shopkeeper is reporting his income for tax purposes. But you are required to take the receipt to be sure the proprietor has rung it up on his cash register tape for the tax authorities. Once in a very great while a police officer will stop someone at the door of a shop and ask to see it. There is, in theory, a fine of £300,000 for not having it, but I have never known of an Italian cop who would enforce such a penalty on a tourist. The same is true for riding a bus without punching your own ticket in the machine at the back door, a process known as *convalidazione*.

Note that Italians use commas for decimal points, and points to separate the zeros in numbers of more than a thousand. Thus 1.000,375 is equal to one thousand and three-eighths. 2,500 would be a three-place decimal expression for two and a half. The problem doesn't come up often since the diminutive value of the lire never requires that prices be quoted in amounts of less than £10, which is around a half cent U.S. Soon prices will be quoted in Euro denomination and the international currency will be in circulation. At this writing one Euro is worth about $1.06.

Our favorite breakfast in Italy is the *cornetto* with the jam *(marmellata)* already on the inside, with a hot cup or glass of *caffé latte*. Orange juice *(succo d'arancia)* will be canned or perhaps frozen, but a *spremuta d'arancia* is fresh-squeezed in quantity from the blood-red Sicilian oranges, and is one of the more delicious treats you will find. Remember that taken standing up at the bar, it will cost you half as much as being served at one of the little tables. On the other hand, if you aim to enjoy your newspaper, you can rent the table for a whole morning for the price of one sit-down cup of coffee. The Paris and Milan English-language *Herald Tribune* is available in the big cities. It is very instructive, but often hard work to decipher an Italian *giornale* such as *La Sicilia* or *La Repubblica*. Most of the other newspapers seem to concentrate rather too exclusively on soccer, *il calcio,* and use a pretty slangy style sheet that may defeat the resource of your pocket dictionary.

Take advantage of shopping for simple things that you

will need while on your trip rather than bringing too much along with you. Men's shirts and ties are a good buy in low-cost places like STANDA (cf. Wal-Mart) or UPIM (cf. J.C. Penney), and are enjoyable souvenirs when you get back home. Of course there are lots of very fashionable and expensive stores in the centers of the larger towns, but in spite of the prices, a $25 necktie in Italy is leagues ahead of a cravat of that price in the United States. Some of the colors common in Italy are absolutely unobtainable in American stores. Most cosmetics are international. Drugstore items are liberally dispensed without prescription, especially antibiotics which require a doctor's order in the U.S. Leather goods and shoes are not always cheap in Italy but they are the finest in the world, and the fashion of ladies' shoes is legendary. Soft, colored leather with miraculously fine stitching is the hallmark of "Made in Italy," a soubriquet pronounced as a title of excellence with the use of the English lexicon and the Italian vowels: "Maideeneetali."

Women's dress in Sicily is, in terms of Italian fashion, relatively conservative. Skirts just now are longer than they are in Bologna or Milan, although the actual amount of thigh covered is a function of age; unattached young women show off plenty of leg. But a deep *scollatura* of the bodice is usually reserved for slightly older women and generally displayed in the evening hours. Dress in church is very much covered up, even for visitors and tourists. *Le nonne,* the grandmothers, all seem to be wearing voluminous black dresses. Tourists have been asked to leave some cathedrals if too much shoulder, bosom or leg is visible. Wearing blue jeans tags you as a tourist, presumably a rich American. Even in hot weather, men never wear shorts unless they are German tourists. I usually travel in spring or autumn and find that wearing a black blazer (with plain buttons) is comfortable. I usually purchase an Italian hat at the beginning of the trip, as well as a couple of brilliant yellow Italian silk cravats. My costume and a certain bespectacled academic air has been rewarded in a number of hotels and restaurants by my being addressed as "Dottore" and once or twice, much to my delight, as "Professore." *Dottore e Dottoressa* are in fact proper terms of address for anyone with any graduate degree, MA as well as PhD. Everyone in this country loves titles, both to bestow and to receive, so don't be shy about making a dinner reservation for yourself and *la Dottoressa* if you deserve it.

Italian barbers and hairdressers *(barbiere e parrucchiere)* are surely the finest in the world. While you are there, take the opportunity to have one of these real professionals do you over. Watch your pronunciation and gender: *cappello* is a hat, which you don't want cropped; *capello* is one hair; *capelli* is the whole head of hair and what you want to have cut *(tagliati)* or perhaps given a trim: *Dammi una spuntatina, per favore, non troppo corti!* (give a trim please, not too short!).

Do learn a bit of Italian. You will be fussed over and encouraged at every attempt to express yourself in the local language. All Sicilians speak very clear standard Italian, partially as the result of Mussolini's effective attempt to stamp out Sicilian as the local or home language two generations ago. There are lots of good phrase books around in good bookstores, but I would urge you not to depend on their transliteration of Italian into phonetic English. This will quickly get in your way and, since Italian is easy to pronounce, you will soon be able to do without it.

For a pocket dictionary, I would suggest the *Larousse,* which has a good plastic binding and thin paper. Its size is a bit limited for working through a magazine text, but it gives lots of useful examples of the words it defines. The *Oxford Italian Minidictionary* is much more comprehensive and although a bit chubby, will fit in a pocket. For a more complete vocabulary get the Penguin paperback dictionary, *The Concise Cambridge Italian Dictionary,* by Barbara Reynolds. Although too big for the pocket *(non tascabile),* it includes a resumé of Italian grammar and good tables of irregular verb forms. This little volume is really nearly as complete as anything short of the ten-pound *HarperCollins Sansoni,* which is the scholar's lexicon. Reading advertisments of American products in Italian magazines is good linguistic practice. Among Italian publications on all newsstands, note *Donna Moderna.* Written and edited for a unisex readership, it is an excellent general magazine that covers a variety of topics from psychology and childrearing to home ownership, finance, sex and horoscopes. Most men's magazines are less satisfactory, being usually too concentrated on sports, sex and automobiles. Contemporary Italian journalese is a bit slangy, and some of the words are not in the standard dictionaries. On the other hand, they use a lot of borrowed English mixed in with the Italian.

Don't stint on guidebooks. In comparison with the price of the trip they are a small and invaluable investment. Get the *Blue Guide* and the *Lonely Planet: Italy* as the minimum. *Let's Go Italy* is more up-to-date than either (being revised annually) and has wonderfully breezy advice from the young travelers of the Harvard University student services. Older travelers might want to select from the most expensive hotels they list, but all are clean and safe. Some of the older and more famous guidebook publishers concentrate too much on the four- and five-star hotels. For description, maps and general information, the *Touring Club of Italy* guide is excellent. If you have room for only one book, take the *Lonely Planet: Italy*. Most hotels will have a desk copy of a comprehensive catalogue of all the hotels in the province, giving facilities, prices, official rating in stars, and the phone and fax numbers for making a reservation. The desk clerk will help you or do it for you.

Don't by any means limit yourself to the periods of time or selection of places among so many sites that are or are not mentioned here. Make your own tour, and you will almost surely find delights unknown to us.

Shop about for a good fare to Sicily. Our travel agent was able to get us to Rome and back for less than $650 each. From there to Palermo was a round trip of $136. You may be able to do better if you start early in the right season. If you are using your Frequent Flyer miles, you should allow lots of lead time to be sure of booking that Rome flight.

So, if you have visited Rome and Florence or Venice and

are looking to broaden your experience with a less crowded tour of the south, do not be timid or anxious as a result of those tales of crime in this island in the sun. Sicily has fewer pickpockets than Rome. It is a lovely country, redolent of history, equipped with excellent tourist facilities, perhaps somewhat less threatening or dangerous than major American cities. There is much to see and savor here.

Buon viaggio!

ABOUT THE AUTHOR

David Hume took to travelling after a long and busy career as headmaster of Saint David's School in New York City. But the need to teach stayed with him after retirement, and he instructs while he describes the places in southernmost Italy that he and his wife Cathy have visited.

The Humes divide their time between Connecticut and North Carolina. David Hume's first book was *Blueberry: A Boat of the Connecticut Shoreline;* and *Towns of the Renaissance: Travellers in Northern Italy.*